BFI Modern Classics

Rob White
Series Editor

BFI Modern Classics is a series of critical studies of films produced over the last three decades. An array of writers explore their chosen films, offering a range of perspectives on the dominant art and entertainment medium in contemporary culture. The series gathers together snapshots of our passion for and understanding of recent movies.

Also Published

Amores Perros
Paul Julian Smith

The Exorcist (revised 2nd edition)
Mark Kermode

The Idiots
John Rockwell

L.A. Confidential
Manohla Dargis

(see a full list of titles in the series
at the back of this book)

Heat

Nick James

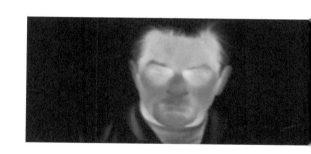

To Kate and Cora

THE BRITISH FILM INSTITUTE
Bloomsbury Publishing Plc
50 Bedford Square, London, WC1B 3DP, UK
1385 Broadway, New York, NY 10018, USA
29 Earlsfort Terrace, Dublin 2, Ireland

BLOOMSBURY is a trademark of Bloomsbury Publishing Plc

First published in Great Britain by Palgrave in 2002
Reprinted 2004, 2009, 2012
Reprinted by Bloomsbury in 2019, 2020, 2022
on behalf of the
British Film Institute
21 Stephen Street, London W1T 1LN
www.bfi.org.uk

The BFI is the lead organisation for film in the UK and the distributor of Lottery funds for film.
Our mission is to ensure that film is central to our cultural life, in particular by supporting and
nurturing the next generation of filmmakers and audiences. We serve a public role which covers
the cultural, creative and economic aspects of film in the UK.

Series design by Andrew Barron &
Collis Clements Associates

A catalogue record for this book is available from the British Library.

A catalog record for this book is available from the Library of Congress.

ISBN: PB: 978-0-8517-0938-3
ePDF: 978-1-8387-1610-3
eBook: 978-1-8387-1609-7

Series: BFI Film Classics

Typeset in Italian Garamond and Swiss 721BT by D R Bungay Associates, Burghfield, Berks
Printed and bound in Great Britain

To find out more about our authors and books visit www.bloomsbury.com
and sign up for our newsletters.

Contents

Acknowledgments

This book would not have been possible without the generous and copious aid of my friend and L.A. spy Manohla Dargis, the advice of Vicky Wilson, the research assistance of Paramjit Rai, Christen Lumen and Jonny Bug, Miles Ogborn, and the painstaking editorial encouragement and support of Rob White and his colleagues, not to mention my own at *Sight and Sound*.

Michael Mann, Al Pacino and Robert De Niro on the coffee-shop set

1 *Heat* – A Bully of a Film

I'd like to know what's behind that grim look on your face.
Diane Venora's Justine to Al Pacino's Vincent Hanna

It was in 1996, at the Warner West End cinema (now the Warner Village) on Leicester Square, that *Heat* was previewed for the UK magazine press and I saw it for the first time. I want to recall the circumstances of that screening because *Heat*, as one of its characters might say, 'goes deep with me'. Its treatment of work, destiny and male identity – themes rehearsed with fierce solemnity by its two stars Robert De Niro and Al Pacino – moves me to a stronger degree than anything in most of the art-house films of the 1990s. Yet this admiration for *Heat* is not easy to justify, not so much because the film is a violent portrait of a criminal crew and their relentless cop pursuer, one that celebrates machismo when I hope I'm usually looking for a cinema of sensitivity and maturity, but more because, in its ambition to be a tragic crime epic of the plazas, back lots and intersections of L.A., it often comes close to overkill.

Writer-director Michael Mann's script uses a rhetoric of existential motivation that's sometimes so hectoring it's like being prodded

Night train in the mist

incessantly in the chest. Yet this threatening up-closeness is all of a piece with the mood of troubled masculinity. You're meant to be uncomfortable with these men because their directness is defensive, and you can tell that underneath their bravado they are twitchily uncomfortable with themselves. Pomposity and self-righteousness are as much a part of their armoury as automatic weapons.

Another obstacle to *Heat*'s claims to be a modern classic is the script's earlier manifestation in the television movie *L.A. Takedown* (1989). At times, reminders of this network television progenitor – a gaudy come-on to the epic movie's sombre pleasures – make it hard to revere *Heat* as more than an exaggerated heist movie.

But, as I hope I will show, *Heat is* much more than that and in 1996 it thrilled me (and not for the last time). Waiting for the film to start, many of the male reviewers around me were anxious to be impressed. Mann had by then become a respected figure for action buffs, with such cult successes as *Thief* (1981), *Manhunter* (1986) and *The Last of the Mohicans* (1992). The film cognoscenti were also present at the screening: archivists, historians and BBC programmers. As the film started, the high brightness of the projection made it hard to forget those around me. (A friend hadn't shown up. The tension of waiting jangled with the mood of submission.) You could almost hear the fans in black T-shirts muttering, 'Michael, please don't fuck it up.'

I admit, I had a similar predisposition and it may be that an indulgent atmosphere aids the enjoyment of such a grim-faced film, because it helps the viewer to go along with the strident insistence of its two protagonists, the thief and the thief-taker, on the purity of their lethal trades. By five minutes in, the film's dazzling craft had banished all my peripheral anxiety. The bombastic dialogue seemed only appropriate to the single-minded élan of the project. *Heat*'s opening scenes are so exactly composed, yet so riven with suspense, they envelop the viewer, sealing absolute attention. They are worth describing in detail.

Through flurries of steam a night train glides towards us. It has three headlights like the dots on dice, one above two below, and it bears the legend 'Los Angeles'. The keening string music we hear over the credits and throughout this scene is set at such a low volume it feels as if there's a sound level problem. Then the train brakes screech loud.

The wide-angle reverse shot that succeeds the opening shot reveals an elevated station of elegant recent design, with the train now squeezing away from us to a halt. The shot treats the track lines and the station's contours – pierced from below by a stake-like escalator well – as near-abstract elements. These shots set such a high standard of pictorial quality that already the viewer is confident of watching an exquisitely designed film. (Any sudden foreground sound throughout this hushed opening sequence has that heightened, intrusive quality experienced in the murmur of early morning.) And symbolically we might be aware that we are about to watch a film about two characters who run along set rails through the night, unable to deviate.

Alighting from the train is Neil McCauley (played by Robert De Niro). Wary but determined, dark hair neat and sleek, goatee beard trimmed very close, he is wearing a grey boiler suit with the collar turned up. We see him descend the escalator, which seems unusually steep, his eyes flicking left and right, a folder in his left hand. As he heads for the hospital across the street, an overhead shot registers another abstract element – a road marking in the form of a stubby curved arrow placed centre screen and pointing towards the top right – which McCauley crosses diagonally in the opposite direction. With casual assurance he strides past a statue in the courtyard (a *pietà*, which prefigures the film's ending), through the ER unit, past computer banks and gory surgical scenes in side rooms, and out to the parking bay, where he steals an ambulance. Immense self-control and efficiency are expressed by his every move. His precision mirrors that of the film itself when in its procedural mode: simple, pared-down, Mellevillian action.

In a construction goods yard in bright morning sunlight, a shrewd-looking elderly sales clerk in a crash helmet and pebble-thick glasses lays a casket marked 'explosives' on a desk for his young pony-tailed customer. The customer, Chris Shiherlis (Val Kilmer), shows him an Arizona driving licence and the deal is done.

Vincent and Justine, a well-preserved middle-aged couple (we recognise Al Pacino as Vincent and maybe Diane Venora as Justine), make tentative early morning love in bed in a modern, hi-tech house. Vincent showers and then Justine, enjoying a post-coital cigarette, asks if he's taking her somewhere for breakfast – he can't, he says, because he's meeting 'Bosko'. Justine's pre-teen daughter Lauren (Natalie Portman) is near hysterical because her natural father is half an hour late to pick her up and she can't find her barrettes. Justine tries to calm her, having herself already swallowed a handful of Prozac.

A muscular, long-haired man wearing wrap-around shades and a grubby black T-shirt (Kevin Gage) exits the toilet of a Mexican café and asks at the counter for a drink refill. Seeing a huge green Persill recovery truck pull up, he runs towards it and clambers up to the door. The tough-looking driver blocks him and asks him his name. 'Waingro', he says and is let in. He asks the driver, Michael Cheritto (Tom Sizemore), about the 'real tight crew' he's working with today. Cheritto says, 'Stop talking would you slick?' Waingro removes his shades and stares at him as if answering a challenge, but Cheritto doesn't notice.

We see McCauley waiting in the ambulance with Shiherlis beside him. A moustachioed Latino man, Trejo (Danny Trejo), calls on a walkie-talkie from his car: he's tailing the target armoured truck, giving a precise run-down as to when it will appear at the chosen spot. It is seconds away. McCauley switches on the ambulance siren and pulls in front of the truck. Cheritto guns his recovery truck into life. It builds up speed as it runs beneath the freeway. Cheritto's rig slams into the armoured truck with such force it upsets the truck onto its side, shoving a whole row of dealer cars several feet back. There's a moment's pause as a severed strip of the dealer's blue bunting gently descends.

The crew, in metal ice-hockey masks, bulletproof vests and carrying automatic weapons, run to surround the truck, waiting to put a stopwatch on as soon as they hear the police alarm call given out on the radio. Shiherlis (the only one wearing a black mask instead of white) positions an explosive shape charge on the door, stands back and sets it off. The impact shatters the windscreens of the dealer cars. McCauley

McCauley descending

Waingro stares at
Cherrito

The windscreens shatter

The staring guard

McCauley orders the
execution

goes inside and hustles out the three guards whose ears are leaking blood and wax. Waingro guards them while Shiherlis rifles through the packages. Trejo runs a line of tyre-slashers across the street.

Waingro, irritated by the wide-eyed stare of one of the guards, pistol-whips him. 'Cut that out would you slick,' Cheritto tells him, pointing out that the guards can't hear him because their eardrums have burst. As soon as Shiherlis finds the package he runs to the ambulance; the others are about to do the same when Waingro, still spooked by the guard's stare, shoots him dead. A second guard then goes for a concealed pistol and is gunned down. Cheritto has the third unarmed guard in his sights, McCauley nods and Cheritto executes him.

As the crew take off their overalls in the ambulance, McCauley disarms Waingro and demands to know what happened. The tyre shredders take out patrol cars arriving at the scene. A few blocks away the crew abandon the ambulance. Shiherlis sets fire to it with all the costumes, weapons and equipment inside.

What was so remarkable about this in 1996? I was immediately impressed by how seriously Mann took this genre subject and by the expense lavished on the film's look of heightened realism. The criminal crew here seems as efficient and well resourced as a Special Forces military unit but the illusion of plausibility holds. Despite the automatic rifles, bulletproof vests, steel masks and the like, you never feel as if you're watching a James Bond film. The criminals give off an air of businesslike neatness (the psychopathic Waingro excepted). They are yuppie villains, whose tidy approach to armed robbery seems to match the 1990s idea of minimalist chic. None of them displays the overt muscularity common to action-movie heroes and villains of the time. Their use of explosives is discreet: designed expressly to avoid the great orange cinematic explosions that are such a signature in the films of Mann's producer contemporaries such as Don Simpson, Jerry Bruckheimer and Joel Silver. The shape charge on the truck is felt as pressure, shattering eardrums and windscreens, not seen as pyrotechnics – even the torched ambulance belches flame without disintegrating.

There's time amid the finger-snapping rush of a suspenseful heist for Mann to include that one moment of calm when the bunting drifts down.

The sound, movement and editing of this opening sequence is orchestrated exactly to mesh with the surging drama of the signature music – electronically treated strings, played by the Kronos Quartet. You could feel by the second how these scenes were raising audience expectations of the realistic action thriller – not only in the aesthetic terms of scale, design and appropriate restraint, but in suspense terms of timing, firepower and tactics. The throbbing of diesel engines merges with the distorted string drone. Machine-gun bursts seem timed to add percussion. *Heat*'s action moves are grounded in the real but their ambition, invention and stylised violence challenge the thrill-count of even John Woo's fantasy action blockbusters.

The armoured car robbery quickly triggers fateful consequences. The crew make enemies of the bearer bonds' owner, money launderer Roger Van Zant, and of Waingro when they try and fail to kill him for murdering the guard. Cheritto's use of the term 'slick' puts Hanna and his men onto the crew while McCauley the perfectionist is distracted by a love affair. A second robbery is aborted because the cops are watching and a third leads to a bloody denouement.

And yet much of the time *Heat* is a sobering, rather slow action movie: a move-by-move *policier* staged in front of the big canvas of Los Angeles, and based on a true story told to Mann by Chuck Stevens, a former cop who had tracked down and killed a thief he admired professionally in the Chicago of the late 1960s. It is also, of course, fraught with male anxiety about women, work and violence.

This bully of a film hustles you along on its own terms, yet it is also confident enough to throw up contradictions in its wake, to leave a great deal of the interpretation to the viewer. Violent crime film, tragic epic, heist movie, realistic thriller, sobering action movie, *policier*, melodrama – by using all these terms in trying to pin down what I enjoy about *Heat* (and what disturbs me) I have intimated what a slippery behemoth it is to define, much more so than such typical recent Hollywood genre hybrids as *Terminator II: Judgement Day* (1991) or *Natural Born Killers* (1994), which are barely on speaking terms with realism.

This difficulty with *Heat* has been acknowledged elsewhere. J. A. Lindstrom in his *Jump Cut* article '*Heat*: Work and Genre' reports that 'reviewers were curiously uncertain as to what the film was about'.[1] He cites the variance in attempts to categorise *Heat* from the *New York Times*, *Variety*, *Hollywood Reporter*, *L.A. Times* and *Newsweek* reviews. Richard Combs in *Film Comment* goes further, arguing that the film 'gives off a blankness, an indeterminacy, that frustrates interpretation ... it's not easy to delve into, to find significance or resonance in its detail'.[2]

For me, rather than blankness, the obstacle to reading *Heat* is its fulsome ambivalence, its teeming contradictions: the tug-of-war between realism and myth, instinct and perfectionism, politics and pleasure, minimalism and brashness and the aesthetic confusion that attends its great ambition. There have been many complex heist movies about greed, deceit and destiny – Stanley Kubrick's *The Killing* (1956), Jules Dassin's *Rififi* (1955) and Quentin Tarantino's *Reservoir Dogs* (1991) for instance – and slowly unfolding procedural sagas such as Sidney Lumet's *Prince of the City* (1981) and *Q&A* (1990) are forerunners of another sort (although too bound up in courtroom exposition to be close relatives). Lindstrom has traced *Heat*'s thematic concerns back to Raoul Walsh's James Cagney vehicle *White Heat* (1949) and to John Huston's *The Asphalt Jungle* (1950)[3] – which Jean-Pierre Melville claimed had all nineteen variations of his favourite cops and robbers situation in the one film.[4] *Heat* may not add a twentieth but no other film I can think of so audaciously spins out the consequences of armed robbery over so long a screen time, so grippingly. It has flavours all its own, this film, and it may be that the very bombast I complain about is the decisive ingredient in making it a modern classic.

2 Michael Mann – Styling the Real Thing

Of all the ambivalences that make *Heat* such a high-wire act, none is more extreme than the contrast between Mann's desire for a hard factual basis to his films and the gleaming, hyper-real end result. Though his crime scenes are compellingly realistic, there is much about *Heat* that approaches myth at the expense of concrete believability. The sense of these hyperbolic cops and felons as real people, in a real environment, gets obscured as much by the theatricality of the film's speechifying as by the thrills of the action genre – let alone the studied elegance of Dante Spinotti's compositions. Still, as we shall see, Michael Mann does insist on authenticity.

Believing myself that the 'death of the author' has been greatly exaggerated by theorists, and that the intentions of such a notorious perfectionist as Mann are genetically encoded into every frame of *Heat*, my approach is first to look at the director's own assessment of his work. At the same time, in considering how far from pure genre such a hybrid epic can be pushed, curiosity should ensure that I examine as many facets as the film plausibly offers. Some of these may show that, in its effort to contain the authentic within a mythic 'cops 'n' robbers' universe, Mann's vision is sometimes corrupted and made strange even to its author by its own contradictions.

When the film was first released, Mann's strategy was to ward off all attempts at pigeonholing. '*Heat* is a drama not a genre piece,' he told *Interview* magazine.[5] 'The crime story … is initially discrete, then it fuses with the personal stories in the fateful and sometimes doom-laden decisions each person has to make.' Similarly, he told the *Sunday Times*, 'None of us viewed *Heat* as an action movie or genre movie. I deliberately didn't allow the crime story to drive the plot. I wanted to tell a human drama, something like a classical tragedy.'[6] Having seen how indeterminate the reviews were to be about which category *Heat* would fit into, the softness of Mann's own definition suggests he wasn't too sure himself – except for his conviction that the film was more than a genre movie and that it had a tragic dimension. For me *Heat* is mostly an expert crime procedural movie, yet sometimes it achieves a level of dramatic pleasure and complexity beyond such confines. What these aspects are I explore later, but Mann's insistence on *Heat* being both a character piece and 'something approaching a classical tragedy' is revealing as much for its nervousness about the genre tag as for its vaunting artistic claims.

That *Heat* is a personal highpoint in its director's career seems beyond doubt. Mann's exploration of the classical American themes of self-reliance and male romantic angst fires all but one of his feature films up to 1995: *The Jericho Mile* (1979), *Thief*, *Manhunter* and *The Last of the Mohicans* (the exception is *The Keep*, 1983). These themes crackle with much greater intensity in *Heat* than in its predecessors and Mann's experience of decades spent working on police dramas – the television shows *Starsky and Hutch*, *Police Story*, *Crime Story*, *Miami Vice* and others – is branded into its detail. The fact that he shot the script twice, first as *L.A. Takedown* – albeit minus a couple of subplots – underlines its personal significance. And since *Heat*'s release, Mann has, for the time being, left crime drama behind to concentrate on true story films of a different order. *Heat* therefore stands as

Michael Mann during production of *The Keep* (Paramount Pictures Corporation, 1983)

a summary of his concerns at that moment in his career. But what is it about genre that makes him so anxious to avoid the label?

Fierce family origins might make Mann resent being demeaned as a genre director. He grew up in a tough neighbourhood of Chicago. His mother was a local girl; his father a Ukrainian émigré, who had fled the Russian revolution, was wounded in World War II and started a grocery store that struggled along for a while before it was forced out of business by competition.[7] His father would apparently see off any local bully that might set upon his sons. But while it is tempting to construct a psychological profile of Mann from his roughhouse childhood, his schooling seems more likely than anything else to have inculcated his need to be recognised as a serious film-maker. He started dabbling in film while reading English at the University of Wisconsin. He filmed some of the Chicago riots and went to the London International Film School in the mid-60s, partly to dodge military service in Vietnam. The LIFS grounded him in documentary: 'In London there was a heavy emphasis on the craft and technology of film-making, which is exactly what I wanted,' Mann told *Sight and Sound*. 'I was there at the same time as Franc Roddam, Gavin McFadyean and David Hart, a lot of guys who went on to work on *World in Action*.'[8]

He returned to the US in 1971 with this documentary bias already in his pocket, as well as some footage of the 1968 Paris riots that found their way onto the national news. The big break into television cop drama came later, after a long period of not getting hired, but it sealed the realist's conviction. He got work writing episodes of *Starsky and Hutch* through story editor Bob Lewin, who instructed him in matters of structure. He then wrote a pilot for *Vega$*, a private eye series which went ahead without him because, he said, it became 'way too sanitized'. Perhaps the breakthrough assignment was the prestigious show *Police Story*, run by the playwright Liam O'Brien, which included Joseph Wambaugh (a revered L.A. cop-turned-novelist, author of *The Onion Field* and *The Choirboys*) among its contributors. Mann was delighted that each episode 'was based on a real event and you had the policeman whose story it was working with you'.[9] This was before the heyday of *Hill*

Starsky and Hutch
(Spelling–Goldberg
Productions, 1975–9)

Street Blues (which began in 1981) and *Cagney and Lacey* (which started in 1982) when reality cop shows with an anti-heroic approach came to dominate the airwaves.

In 1979 Mann became secure and confident enough to tell ABC, his main employers, that he wouldn't do any more writing for them unless he could direct. When they said yes, he took a teleplay by Patrick J. Nolan and rewrote it as a $60,000 television movie, *The Jericho Mile*. Its importance to *Heat* is manifold.

It's here that we meet our first typical Mann protagonist, Rain Murphy (Peter Strauss), a convicted killer and a gifted athlete. Trying to achieve Olympic standard amid the brutal caprice of US prison life, he dedicates himself to a gruelling training routine. When a friendship ensnares him in a dispute between the racial gangs, his struggle becomes the solitary one of all Mann's protagonists – he can only achieve his personal triumph by breaking free of all attachments. Made for the ABC movie-of-the-week slot, *The Jericho Mile* was shot entirely within the walls of Folsom State Penitentiary. Actors mixed with 28 convicts in speaking parts and 658 more as extras. The exercise yard was not only the site of Murphy's personal struggle it was also carefully divided racial turf. *The Jericho Mile* shows that Mann was already an expert at constructing a vivid social arena against which to play out a personal drama of pain and deliverance.

The Jericho Mile (ABC Circle Films, 1979)

'People want reality in movies today,' Mann insisted soon afterwards. 'They want the real thing, real people, real locations. They see the real thing on their television news shows. They want a movie to look real.'[10] Folsom provided Mann with a small-scale model for society, with brute force and barter the only modes of survival, and his experience there feeds directly into *Heat*: Neil McCauley's rap sheet reports seven years in Folsom, three of them in 'the hole'; Shiherlis was clearly there with him, as was Breedan, the parolee; and Waingro tells the crooked bartender he's from 'Folsom B-Wing, a cowboy looking for anything heavy'.

Mann's insistence on accurate research would intensify over his next three films, gaining him a reputation for exactitude among film crews that was often more grudgingly respectful than flattering. *The Jericho Mile*'s critical success made him a name, giving him the power to direct almost anything he wanted. His next film, *Thief*, involved his friend Chuck Adamson, the policeman whose personal anecdote would inspire the script for *Heat* and who would later become a writer on *Crime Story*. Mann met Adamson in the early 1970s when he was the Head of Investigation for the Sheriff of Clark County, the municipal authority of Las Vegas. He introduced Mann to the sophisticated criminal John Santucci, who supplied much true-to-life detail for *Thief* – though the script originated as an adaptation of Frank Hohimer's book *The Night*

Invaders. (Another cop, William Handhart, who is waiting as I write to be sentenced for a number of professional jewel heists committed since his retirement from the force, has also been a close Mann adviser.[11])

Thief has the most hardcore of all Mann's protagonists: Frank (James Caan), a high-line thief so true to his lights he sacrifices his entire universe just to maintain his independence. When a local mobster forces Frank to work for him and then short-changes him after a job, Frank's revenge is absolute: he sends his gently wooed girlfriend and their adopted child away for ever, burns down his own used car dealership, car by car, and executes the mobster and his entire gang without mercy. From the perspective of *Heat*, *Thief* is important for illustrating the terrifyingly simple attitude to life that Neil McCauley says he learned in Folsom: 'Jimmy McIlhenny in the yard used to say if you want to be making moves on the street, have no attachments, have nothing in your life that you can't walk out on in 30 seconds flat if you spot the heat around the corner.' Frank acts out this dictat to the full.

Like *Heat*, *Thief* is in thrall to the technology of thievery. We experience, with growing fascination, the complex planning and handling of heavy equipment. It's the kind of crime film that wears its research like a shoulder flash on grimy overalls. It makes sure you know that robbery is sweated work, requiring strength, nerve, concentration and dangerous machines. Mann's admiration for Frank is unambiguous. He portrays him as a near-noble figure ruined by the criminal system. This attitude of respect, towards people whom Mann is also always careful to label as psychotic in interviews, is essential to our understanding of *Heat*. Despite the gunplay, the tenor of the film is always one of compassionate understanding.

With the release of *Thief*, Mann spelled out his reality-based method: 'My way of working with a project involves accumulating a tremendous amount of detailed, "soft" information. I have to feel the whole subculture. I like being able to go into very hostile environments and figure them out, operate from within them.'[12] *Thief* is the closest of Mann's features to verité (although not very close). It also shares the funky urban grain of such 1970s underworld movies as *Mean Streets* (1973), *The French Connection* (1971) and *Shaft* (1971). Elements of the

highly designed visual style for which Mann would soon become notorious are present but relatively subdued.

In the director's next feature, *Manhunter*, an adaptation of Thomas Harris's novel *Red Dragon*, 'style' becomes a more pressing issue. Someone as fascinated by criminal psychology as Mann was sure to find this elegant serial killer thriller irresistible, especially its phenomenal secondary character, the infamous sociopath Hannibal 'The Cannibal' Lecter. In *Manhunter*, whose subject is remarkable men who go beyond the rational to achieve their goals, Mann's fascination with the mythic potential of his characters overshadows his allegiance to the real. As usual, Mann conducted an 'immense amount' of pre-production research into police procedures and serial killers. 'For some while I talked to a guy locked away in a California mental institution for life, and then I also spent a lot of time with the FBI's Behavioral Science Unit.'[13]

Thief (United Artists, 1981): Frank's safe-breaking machinery and his act of self-destruction

What counts most in *Manhunter* from the *Heat* perspective is the relationship between the uncannily brilliant Lecter (Brian Cox) and the 'empath' cop Will Graham (William Petersen) – who has the ability to think like a serial killer and to see things from their point of view. Their supernatural kinship (Graham caught Lecter but was badly injured in the process) presages that between Hanna and McCauley: Hanna's ability to think like a thief is along the same lines as Graham's empathy with serial killers. Graham is encouraged by the insidious Lecter to see himself as special because of his insight, as one of the elect allowed by their general superiority to behave as they please, pursuing, if you will, a Nietzschean 'will to power'.

Will Graham and Hannibal Lecter take their place alongside Frank and Rain Murphy in Mann's pin-up book of outsiders, his compendium of driven, hyper-perceptive types who confront the problems of

Manhunter (De Laurentiis Entertainment, 1986): imagery of cages and bars

contemporary living in the 'urban jungle' by reverting to instinct (an idea that takes a lot of directorial faith to sustain). The difference from Frank is that Graham and Lecter are more than human, as indeed is the home-invading serial killer on the loose whom Graham needs Lecter's help to catch: Francis Dollarhyde (Tom Noonan), the 'Red Dragon'. With its more expressive, spooky scenes inspired by Dollarhyde's derangement, and its cooler antiseptic settings mirroring Lecter's tidy calculation, Mann's treatment of Harris's novel set loose his talent for creating transcendent moods and a thoroughgoing image system.

Manhunter has a design scheme as rigorously planned out as Hitchcock's *North By Northwest* (1959), with its fascination for the parallel lines of Renaissance perspective. Frame after frame of *Manhunter* insists on the imagery of cages and bars: from the opening shot of fenced-in turtles, to the chairs and window frames of Graham's modernist beach house, to the actual bars on Lecter's cell that seem somehow to be shared by Graham when looked at from Lecter's perspective. These shots of a rational, boxed-off, clinically clean world of suppression are contrasted with Dollarhyde's murky house of love and death, of low lamps and big Blake posters.

Manhunter was a very glossy product for 1986. Its hi-tech look was matched at the time only by William Friedkin's cops-'n'-coke thriller *To Live and Die in L.A.* (1985), which also starred William Petersen and looks rather like a Mann film – Pauline Kael described it as 'gaudy pulp'.[14] *Manhunter* is beloved of cult film fans for its cool intensity and for Cox's measured, subtly sinister portrayal of Lecter. But it also gained Mann a reputation for visual flash with which he has never become comfortable. 'The main trouble is Mr. Mann's taste for overkill,' wrote Walter Goodman in the *New York Times*, 'attention keeps being directed away from the story to the odd camera angles, the fancy lighting, the crashing music.'[15] Richard Combs wrote in the *Monthly Film Bulletin* that *Manhunter* 'courts the danger, in a film which has so thoroughly "glossed" its own subject in the process of detaching itself from genre, of making something which is more resonant at the surface than it can ever be underneath'.[16] These critiques are inspired arguably by Mann's own exactitude. 'Everything in that film is there by design,' he told *Time Out*. 'Nothing is accidental. Every prop, down to the utensils and artefacts in the killer's kitchen, is there to give a sense of unease, distortion, insanity. The colours, camera-angles, locations: all there to create dread.'[17] Here authenticity itself becomes style, where a perfectionist's concern for psychological symbolism begets the hyper-real in a cinema of precisely framed big gestures.

The typecasting of Mann as an empty stylist (rather in the way the French directors of the '*cinéma du look*', Luc Besson and Jean-Jacques Beineix, were treated at the time) had begun with the sudden hiatus in his career that led him, in 1984, back to television as the creator and executive producer of *Miami Vice*. He retreated from features after *The Keep* – a bizarre Nazis-meet-the-supernatural tale – turned out to be a financial disaster. This expensive movie flopped badly, earning just $1.2 million, and is not worth dwelling on here since its relevance to *Heat* is marginal. Suffice to say it put Mann in a situation where a return to television became attractive.

'I kinda tripped sideways and accidentally fell into *Miami Vice*,' said Mann. 'The earlier work I did on television was simply a means to an end ... The sheer producing part of television I don't enjoy at all.'[18] The script for the pilot was such an obvious commercial winner that he wanted to make it into a movie. The company refused but, though he never directed an episode, he became the series auteur, inventing a candy-coloured

Miami Vice (Universal Television, 1984–90)

Miami of glitz and guts for his two protagonists, vice cops Crockett and Tubbs (Don Johnson and Philip Michael Thomas), in their war of attrition against the cocaine trade. They wore designer suits, often white or cream, with the sleeves rolled up and T-shirts underneath, and loafers with no socks. They drove expensive fast cars and motorboats – Sonny Crockett even lived aboard a sailing boat – and they drove to a pounding soundtrack of rock and pop hits. No matter how light-heartedly pulpy the intention, *Vice* was taken very seriously by a lot of people and Mann was stuck with the 'designer' label of looks over content. 'Impact in *Miami Vice*', said *Film Comment*'s Richard T. Jameson, 'is first and foremost a matter of style.'[19] Mann seemed to become all the more anxious about the validation authenticity could give him. 'I detest style,' he told *Time Out* when *Heat* was released. 'Style is simply gratuitous form with no content; it's for commercials. So I don't think of myself as a stylist. My attitude is that the audience is a human organism sitting there in a dark room, and that everything affects the way people feel and perceive a movie.'[20] He put it more bluntly to *Sight and Sound*: 'Style only gets you seven minutes of attention.'[21]

The problem for Mann is that he understands too well film's ineluctable tendency to mythologise. You can see it in the symbolic nature of Frank's rage in *Thief* as he torches every car in his dealership lot – an event that stretches plausibility. Mann's skill with a kinetic, lavish, widescreen cinema came to fruition in *Manhunter*. But just as the active killer Dollarhyde is allowed to take on his own mythic estimate of himself – with his giant stature and the mask that half hides his bullet-shaped head and pitiless eyes – Mann too became his own monster: a thoroughgoing master of an enveloping, immersive cinema. Already there was something curious about so effects-driven a film-maker (in the sense of filmic effects rather than special effects) being so wedded to the details of real life, for realism is not really the level at which we experience a Michael Mann film.

And yet, it's arguable that the differing forms of cinema realism are merely expressions of different national traditions of what constitutes the representation of the real. In the UK we tend to think of grainy, television-scale dramas about social ills as our touchstone of realism. For Mann it is more about getting authentic physical and psychological detail right and ripe for its blowing up into mainstream cinema entertainment. As we shall see, even our documentary ideas of realism are becoming infected with the language of the crime film. But watching *Thief*, *Manhunter*, *The Last of the Mohicans* or indeed *Heat*, we are not, in the end, telling ourselves that these are real events, however well observed. Maybe that's why Mann subsequently turned to the ultimate validation of the 'true story' tag with *The Insider* (1999) and *Ali* (2002), so that he can be as imaginative as he likes and still have the audience believe that what he shows them is related to how it was.

Mann has said that he has no talent for making things up and that in any case reality provides a much better basis for stories (Ridley Scott recently said much the same thing when defending *Black Hawk Down*, 2001, and playwright David Hare has also argued that in the twenty-first century the best art is conceived in response to the real world[22]). 'I try and get to that [authenticity] through preparation,' he says, 'doing a lot of work on the milieu of a film: prowling L.A. at night, talking to crime victims and their relatives, finding out what really moves seasoned, callous homicide cops, talking with ex-cons. And what one discovers from that are tiny pieces of authenticity, which are usually more interesting or original than stuff I could make up in a sitting room.'[23]

The director would not deny that he transmutes these elements of deep research into something other than realism – if realism is a representation of mundane daily life. But there's still a tension between the mythic-heroic aspects of his storytelling and the immersive psychological ones. And whether or not his transmutation achieves the combined pity and terror of tragedy, or should even wish to, remains to be seen. What is certain is that *Heat* reverberates with echoes of Mann's other films, and with themes that have concerned him for a long time. This, of course, makes him as much of an auteur as a Bergman or a Bresson.

3 'The action *is* the juice'

'Chuck Adamson … shot and killed the real Neil McCauley, in Chicago in 1963,' Mann told *Time Out*.

What was most striking about it was that he'd met McCauley; quite by accident, they'd had coffee together. And Chuck had respected this guy's professionalism – he was a really good thief, which is exciting to a detective, and he tried to keep any risks to a minimum – but at the same time he was a cold-blooded sociopath who'd kill you as soon as look at you – if *necessary*. Anyway, Chuck was going through some crises in his life, and they wound up having one of those intimate conversations you sometimes have with strangers. There was a real rapport between them; yet both men verbally recognised one would probably kill the other. And subsequently Chuck was called to an armed robbery, saw McCauley coming out, and there was a chase: Chuck came round a corner, McCauley came up with his gun but it misfired, and Chuck shot him six times. But it was the intimacy, the mutual rapport that became the nucleus of the film.[24]

That the complex saga of *Heat* could have been spun from this short reminiscence is remarkable. Admiration and respect between opposing men of violence is the central theme in *Heat*, but the typical Western scene in which enemies pay tribute to one another face to face on horseback barely gives a clue to the complexities of sympathy and despair here. Neil McCauley and Vincent Hanna (the fictional Adamson) go beyond chivalric ceremony to admit their mutual frailty. A great deal of screen time will be occupied by their questioning of their career choices, especially through their romantic attachments to women. But before we get to their home lives, we had better understand what kind of men they are, what kind of world they operate in, and how their professional relationships work.

At the moment where we left them, during the aftermath of the armoured car robbery, neither McCauley nor Hanna knew the other existed (and each remains unaware of the other's specific identity until much later). We've seen McCauley in action and Hanna at home as discreet hard men who wear sharp suits and carry an icy air of gravitas befitting the 1990s. Playing these roles, De Niro and Pacino combine the virtues and vices of various genre archetypes – from true-grit Western heroes to film noir's most implacable villains. But if they seem more real, it's largely because they're playing typical workaholics. *Heat*'s awareness of the politics of work is conscious but Mann has it both ways in the sense that for these men work *is* pleasure – a common 1990s social observation about most of us. Or, as Michael Cheritto puts it when Neil asks him if the final heist is worth the risk, given that he has plenty of money stashed away and a wife to look after him: 'for me the action *is* the juice.'

From the beginning, both protagonists are strong at work but weak at leisure. Take the way we first get to know Hanna. The tentative sex scene at the start of the film, when he's with his wife Justine (with its postscript of Lauren getting hysterical about meeting her father), is the

Tentative sex

one domestic exception in an opening sequence otherwise devoted to thriller plot and action. It is there simply to introduce Vincent Hanna and to indicate his marital problems. At first you think it is working as an extra attention-grabber, but the sex is so balanced between the tender and the perfunctory – shot coyly in evasive glances, as if to avoid any traces of ageing male flesh – it doesn't register at all as a competing sensation to the robbery build-up. Vincent at home is already a pathetic, almost ghostly figure. But shortly we will meet an entirely different being – the cop.

Mann's affinity with men whose work forces them into extreme situations seems a sealed bond – it's there in nearly all his films: in *The Last of the Mohicans* and *Ali* as much as those I've already discussed. From this perspective, the real cop and his nemesis, being determined men of physical courage, living heightened lives outside normal society, can only be fictionalised on an epic scale. *Heat*'s route to its aesthetic is therefore widescreen largesse, the highly polished New Hollywood cinema that multiplex audiences flocked to in the 1980s and 90s. With such industrial means at its disposal, the film can rapidly shift its sense of scale back and forth from, say, the intimate meeting in the coffee house to large set-piece actions that require the backdrop of a terrific landscape – the protean sprawl of Los Angeles – to give the sense of grandeur appropriate to these unique individuals and their (supposedly) unique emotions.

This stretching of a friend/enemy dual connection to a measure where catharsis can only be achieved in death and destruction seems both characteristic of crime movie logic and revealing of how fraught with anxiety about male intimacy crime movies are. The buddy–buddy relationship is valued more highly than any love affair. But male bonding in the profession of violence is such an overwhelming generic trope of recent cinema it's hard to take issue with any one example.

In the aftermath of the robbery come three scenes in which all the fateful loading of the dice that plays out to the end of *Heat* happens: the overhearing of Cheritto's catch-word 'slick', the agreement to deal with the treacherous Roger Van Zant (William Fichtner), and the failure to kill Waingro. In a car park overlooking the towers of Downtown L.A., Neil McCauley delivers the bonds to Nate (John Voight). There is absolute trust between the thief and this grizzled, wise-seeming friend, fence and fixer (much like that between Frank and his dying prison mentor in *Thief*). McCauley is still furious about the killing of the guards but he lets Nate persuade him to look at two new risky but lucrative propositions. First, there's a bank robbery on offer from Kelso, a computer wizard (played by Mann regular Tom Noonan). Second, Nate has a scam to sell the bonds back to their owner, money launderer Van Zant, because he is insured for the theft and will therefore profit. As they part, Nate asks, 'What happened out there?' 'Don't ask,' says McCauley.

From the car park we cut to Lieutenant Hanna of the LAPD's Robbery Homicide division, arriving in his sleek black car at the crime scene. Here Pacino utterly dominates the screen. He does this small skip

Nate and McCauley

Hanna the undead

and swagger redolent of a stage entrance as he exits his car in long shot, scanning the scene. He's radiating a quite phenomenal sense of command for one so compact. His movements seem all the more deliberate because of the waxy look of his face: he's made up like a cadaver. It has to be night, you realise, for is he not one of the undead, prowling around in the dark with his hair gelled back?

We're ideally set for some grandstanding, for Pacino's unique brand of verbal fireworks: the eyeballing and barking necessary for this role seem to encapsulate the mature Pacino's essence. Having listened to details of the crime, Pacino moves into his first oration, making big gestures with his arms like some cross between St Peter in Caravaggio's *Supper at Emmaus* and a traffic cop. His right-hand man Danny Bosko (Ted Levine) – a walrus-mustachioed figure about whom we find out little – is just finishing his summation: 'And it was a million six in bearer bonds and they ignored the loose cash.'

'Because they had no time because they were on a clock,' continues Hanna, 'which means they had our response time to a 2:11, had our air, immobilised it, entered, escaped in under three minutes. It's a good escape route here, you've got two freeways within a quarter of a mile.' Hailing the professionalism of McCauley's crew, Hanna

laments the lack of clues – there's just the one remark overheard by a homeless man in hiding, when Cheritto referred to Waingro as 'slick'. The only other hope for Hanna and his team is if the explosive used is 'exotic' and therefore traceable. Having given out orders for gathering evidence, he's asked by Sergeant Drucker (Mykelti Williamson), 'What's the MO?'

Hanna's reply is one of Pacino's best moments in the film, certainly in terms of brio and timing. (In this scene of a control freak taking over a crime scene, one might read a small parody of how Mann is reckoned to behave on set.) Here Pacino roars his professional appreciation of ruthlessness: 'The MO is that they're good. Once it escalated into a murder beef for all of them after they killed the first two guards, they didn't hesitate, popped guard number three because … what difference does it make, why leave a living witness – drop of a hat, these guys will rock and roll.'

This final remark initiates Hanna's curiosity about a man he does not yet know. Much later, when the two finally meet, Hanna will still seem to have the bigger need to commune than McCauley because De Niro plays McCauley in a much less demonstrative mode than his co-star. McCauley's Zen-like acceptance of daily events would handle meeting Hanna without any great excitement.

So far McCauley has been all action: an almost mute figure intent on nothing but his tasks. He enjoys as much authority over his crew as

Hanna does over his men and he is ready to kill at a moment's notice. De Niro's thief is a portrayal of ruthlessly efficient self-interest but it explores few of the traits one expects of a gang boss – only the constant suppression of anger and the visible dyspepsia. The actor's tone is dour but quiet, like the businessman he dresses to resemble (though his extreme ex-con's neatness would give him away in such company).

His next scene shows us that he will act violently when it suits him, and it also demonstrates some differences between the police and thieves. Admiration for the tightness and loyalty of McCauley's crew is a major appeal of *Heat*. They're like a group of dedicated Samurai (and the echoes between Westerns and Japanese Samurai film reverberate here as much as in many other films). Hanna's officers are also loyal but more laid back. While Hanna paces out the scene, they listen attentively, but they have a relaxed air of good fellowship about them. These are men of easy fraternal bonds for whom a crime scene holds no terrors. Standing about, cocksure in their suits, they look as if they own the streets.

Cutting to Shiherlis, Cheritto, Trejo and Waingro waiting at a truck stop café, we notice two sets of behavioural contrasts: first, between the regular crew and Waingro, and second, between the crew's teamwork and the cop fellowship we've just witnessed. Waingro is trying to normalise the situation after he has needlessly killed the guard by asking if anyone wants any of the pie he's eating. He is studiously ignored. While Trejo disappears, seemingly to 'the can', Shiherlis and Cheritto behave like watchful automata, entirely in concert with each other, ready at a glance to do McCauley's bidding. Their synchronicity helps us to admire, respect and even like them. They are on the alert, scoping the background, watching the exits and positioning themselves to box in Waingro. McCauley arrives and sits next to Waingro who says of the murdered guard, 'I had to get it on, man.' Instantly McCauley grabs him by his hair and smacks his head into the table and against the window a few times. McCauley explains that he's redivided the initial 'take' because he wants to pay off 'this muthafucker' in full now.

They exit to the car park and again McCauley grabs Waingro in a painful hold and leads him by the nose to a spot next to the plastic-lined

open trunk of Trejo's car, where he topples him to the floor, pistol-whips him seemingly unconscious and is about to shoot him dead when Cheritto spots a patrol car. They wait and watch for few seconds until the car is gone and then find Waingro has somehow disappeared.

Unlike the police, the thieves are never on their own turf, never at ease. In that sense they're closer to Mann's usual outsider figures, whose senses remain heightened at all times – for instance Hawkeye (Daniel Day-Lewis) and his Mohawk companions in *The Last of the Mohicans* – than the cops are. There's only one obvious exception: Hanna. His men remain fairly anonymous in comparison to McCauley's crew. Which means that *Heat* isn't quite the even match that Chuck Adamson's anecdote suggests. Like any good crime film, its main sympathies lie with the criminals, and it forces the representative of the law to opt out from society himself if he wants to catch them.

Watchful automata (top); leading Waingro by the nose (below)

4 Blue Interlude

A mirror-like surface floats in the foreground of a bare unlit room, reflecting what's beyond it: a set of glass sliding doors that open onto a concrete balcony with a fuzzy view of the night-time ocean. The sea is intensely blue, flooding the room with blue (I don't know what blue, lighter than Matisse blue or Yves Klein blue, but just as intense, and almost phosphorescent). After a moment, we know the object is the top of a glass table. Into the frame comes a hand in close-up. It casts a set of keys and a chunky automatic pistol onto the table. As the male figure walks to the window we see only his legs. The gun on the table remains a sleek-tooled object floating near-abstract in the foreground. And then the camera tilts upwards, plunging the table out of sight and we recognise Neil McCauley's dark-etched silhouette. He is stooping, with one foot raised on a ledge and his left arm leaning onto the doorframe. It's an immaculately framed image of an immaculately turned-out man.

Then, in close-up, we see the surface of McCauley's left cheek. The camera pulls focus, melting the cheek and bringing the frothing ocean into sharp relief before we go back to the long shot and McCauley walks out of the frame.

And that's it. That's the scene that comes straight after the failed attempt to kill Waingro, the scene that marks the transition from pure thriller procedure to interior drama. No scriptwriting guru would ever condone such a scene because it adds nothing to the forward motion of the story and it says nothing that we don't know already. That McCauley is a solitary man is already established. Nevertheless it's a gorgeous moment in the enjoyment of *Heat*. There's a strong identification between the aesthetic of the film and the thief's own tastes. He lives in a very expensive, unfurnished, modernist beach house – and yes, the symbolism is corny, but acutely effective.

This is the first interior of a tour of living quarters and its blueness is important in setting the mood for what comes in the next few scenes. Blue in Mann's colour-coding is not only the hue of melancholy, it also stands for romantic love – the other blue-flooded room in his canon is

The gun (top); an immaculately turned-out man (middle); the blue-flooded room in *Manhunter* (bottom)

the bedroom of Will Graham's idyllic family beach house in *Manhunter*, the one that is nevertheless a cage of sorts. *Heat* slows down now. Dissatisfaction invades the characters. The discontent between lovers that we are about to experience is everyday slice-of-life stuff, but it has a slightly forced cosmic edge.

Mann's 'human drama' gives unusual prominence in a crime film to women as domestic partners. They are there not only to show us, in romantic and sexual terms, what the men have to lose, but also to challenge their inadequacy and to thwart their excesses. It's an awkward fit at first because of the common Hollywood tension of needing to show women in terms of self-empowerment while at the same time corralling them in essentially nurturing roles. Mann's efforts to weave domestic conflict into a thriller sometimes feel like a restraint on the action. And yet, the closer the film builds to its climax, the more essential as building blocks to *Heat*'s payoff these scenes become.

By the time McCauley's comrades have failed to kill Waingro we know each of them only slightly. The way Mann treats most of the crew's domestic lives follows the example of classic crime films like *The Killing*, *Rififi* and *Asphalt Jungle*. These films tend to sketch quick details – such as a sick child in need of expensive healthcare or a small boy who adores his dad without knowing he's a hoodlum – merely to grant some swift sympathy. *Heat* treats Trejo in much the same way. In a few scenes time we will see Anna (Begonya Plaza), his attractive wife, enjoying the birthday celebration for Elaine (Susan Traylor), Michael Cheritto's wife. We see this only so that Anna's subsequent off-screen rape and murder can have its proper impact. Elaine doesn't feature in more than a couple of scenes herself.

Chris Shiherlis and his wife are the exception. The young thief's home life with Charlene (Ashley Judd) and their baby Dominick forms its own subplot of love and betrayal. So far we've seen him as a pale, wired explosives expert who acts coolly in a crisis. Now we see his home (glass-and-steel modernism again) with its pool and we meet the vibrant, hardheaded Charlene, who is complaining because he's only brought home $8,000 dollars from a bank raid. (It's only the initial payment and Shiherlis has had to pay off his considerable gambling debts.) She tells him, 'It's not worth the risk, as in risk versus reward baby.' He's in a hurry to go out and doesn't want to hear this. 'There is no point talking to you,' she says, 'because all you are is a child growing older.' 'What does that mean?' he asks. 'It means that we're not making forward progress like real grown-up adults because I'm married to a gambling junkie who won't listen.'

Quick to explode (like his *matériel*), Chris hurls a glass at a picture frame and tells Charlene, 'Leave the bank book and the car keys on the table on your way out the door.' Her firm reply is a little indistinct but it sounds like, 'You can keep that other crap but Dominick would go with me.' (So prepared was I by Mann's script notes for the women in *Heat* to use therapy-speak that the first few times I watched this scene I thought she was saying, 'You can keep that other crap but dominant won't go with me'!) Chris is about to threaten her again when the baby starts crying. Then he storms off into the night in his low-slung sports car, where he can hit the lights and burn off his anger. Luxury is obviously important to this couple but not as important as their baby son. Though Charlene is as inscrutable as many other women in Mann's films, we can see that her concern with money is more about security for her baby than greed.

The tour of the women and homes continues, each signifying status and fragile anchorage in the real world. Hanna is in his car, finding out by cellphone that the explosive cannot be traced and that his snitch, Albert Torena (Ricky Harris), has not called. At home Justine confronts him with blanked-out anger. Hanna is just starting to disparage Lauren's father because he didn't show up when Justine says, 'She's not OK and neither am I. I made dinner for us four hours ago.' In her Audrey Hepburn combination of black pants and sweater, Justine always looks more capable and designer-bright than her use of Prozac and, later, dope would have us believe. She's also quick to challenge Hanna. 'Every time I try to maintain a consistent mood between us you withdraw,' she tells him. He counters with a description of 'Three dead bodies on a sidewalk off Venice Boulevard' but falters, as if to admit his mistake in not at least calling her. This is a relationship built slowly and shakily on carefully earned trust between people who have 'been burned' before. Hanna is

not really at home in Justine's house (which was bought by her ex-husband), he has only a quasi-guest status, even though they are married.

Suspicion and hostility between the sexes even spills over into the next scene, one of romance, in which McCauley meets a young woman at a café lunch counter. She asks him about a book on metals he's just bought (*Stress Fractures In Titanium*). He bristles: why does she want to know? When she explains that she works in the bookstore and has seen him there many times, he relaxes and puts out his hand. And here we get a long look at the girl (played by Amy Brenneman) as she decides whether or not to accept his handshake: she's awkward, shy, and altogether unready for a sexual encounter. She introduces herself as Eady, an aspiring graphic designer. He tells her he's a salesman in metals.

Soon they are on the balcony of her apartment enjoying a panoramic view of the lights of L.A., while Terje Rypdal's guitar wrings

Charlene: 'All you are is a child growing older' (top); Justine in black (below)

pathos out of the high notes. She tells him her family history, originally 'Scots Irish'. He says his mother's dead, he didn't know his father, and that he's got a brother somewhere. They're strangers giving too much information too soon. De Niro plays Neil McCauley as a sad, introverted romantic who seems to have found someone as halting at the social niceties as himself. He's very restrained, as if holding in great pain. 'City of lights', he says, gazing down at the winking sea beneath him. 'In Fiji they have these irridescent algae that come out once a year in the water. That's what it looks like out there.' 'You been there?' asks Eady. 'No,' he says, 'but I'm going someday.' This is as close to a sly joke as *Heat* gets, but the sheer bathos of McCauley's sincerity kills the chuckle before it's born. De Niro has acquired such a sense of menace over years of playing psychopaths he can suggest a world of terror in one gesture. Here he's being tender but tense, as you'd expect of an ex-con. Yet

A long look at Eady (top); 'In Fiji they have these irridescent algae' (bottom)

Brenneman's Eady remains fragile, barely out of her shell, never really much more than a personal-ad description ('Quiet Artistic Woman Seeks Cathartic Psychopath'?), though she is, as you would expect, lovely to look upon.

Posing protagonists against an overwhelming landscape is a regular motif for Mann. McCauley's apartment overlooks the sea, as did Graham's in *Manhunter*, and Lowell Bergman's (Pacino again) in *The Insider*, and there is the extraordinary climax to *The Last of the Mohicans*, on a high rock, with a backdrop of awesome mountains, where the young Mohawk brave dies and the heroine's younger sister commits suicide by jumping after him. It's perhaps a simple way of introducing existential fragility to such ambitions as visiting Fiji one day when your profession is so risky as that of an armed bank robber.

McCauley meets Eady half an hour into the film. Structurally it's the 'turning point' for his character, the moment when he lets a world of possibilities into the monk's cell of his mind. This is how Mann sets him up to be a tragic character. As in many crime dramas, McCauley will not be able to resist the one last job that will make his life secure. 'At bottom, the gangster is doomed because he is under the obligation to succeed, not because the means he employs are unlawful ...' says Robert Warshow in 'The Gangster as Tragic Hero'.

No convention of the gangster film is more strongly established than this: it is dangerous to be alone. And yet the very conditions of success make it impossible not to be alone, for success is always the establishment of an individual pre-eminence that must be imposed on others ... The gangster's whole life is an effort to assert himself as an individual, to draw himself out of the crowd, and he always dies because he is an individual.[25]

McCauley has a fantasy of escaping the fold not only of society, but even the society of his own gang, yet to achieve that he must trust his own instincts, instincts that would, by his own rules, preclude the fantasy in the first place.

Male–female relations in *Heat* therefore evince their own structural weaknesses. The women in *Heat* are aware of their place in society and of the responsible communal decisions that can be taken to resist bad luck, whereas the men try to avoid attachments that might impede their instinct. In their desire to stay sharp, the men make themselves vulnerable to the circumstance of the moment. 'The commonality of both men is that they know life is short, time is luck,' says Mann. 'Their awareness of the instant of decision is a choice. ("What's it going to be? One Answer. Yes or no. Right now.")'

This dichotomy is what haunts McCauley. Is his affair with Eady a sign of weakness or is it his redemption – a chance to escape the psychopath he's become? As if in answer we now see the nurturing side of McCauley. After meeting with Kelso to discuss the bank job, he finds Shiherlis sleeping on his floor. He calls Charlene to ask her what's wrong and she says, curtly, 'husband and wife stuff'. Over coffee Shiherlis says he thinks she'll leave him. McCauley asks him if he's got someone on the side or if Charlene has. Shiherlis says he has nothing regular and doesn't think she has. McCauley reminds him of the Folsom dictat about having nothing in your life that you can't walk out on. Shiherlis just shrugs and says, 'For me the sun rises and sets with her, man.'

Denial of social responsibility is supposedly McCauley's manifesto: it might make sense of his romance with Eady, based as it is on the lie that he's a salesman, because one can always walk away from a relationship based on a fantasy. However, as a critique of Shiherlis's relationship with Charlene, it might also – if we imagine the closeness of the relationship between the two men in Folsom – be tinged with jealousy. A few scenes later McCauley catches Charlene in a motel room, just after she's waved goodbye to her new lover Marciano. Shoving his finger in her face, he insists that she give Shiherlis one last chance, after which, if it fails, he will set her and Dominick up himself. Despite Eady, despite his paternal air, McCauley, in his dealings with Charlene, acts like her rival. And for a man supposedly primed to walk out on any commitment, he seems now to want to bind people to him. Already we can see that, according to his own rules, McCauley is doomed by his need to tidy up the messes of his crew as much as by his succumbing to the fantasy of escaping with Eady.

In the next scene we see McCauley and the crew back in the arena of action and instinct. The viewer almost shares their sense of relief. We already know that the deal set up by Nate with Van Zant to sell him back his own bearer bonds is a double-cross. As soon as McCauley got off the phone while he was spying on Charlene, the yuppie money launderer said – while handing a note to someone without looking at them – 'I can't have word out on the street that people can steal from me.' So the drop-off scene comes with some anticipation and suspense.

A white pick-up truck rolls slowly across an empty drive-in lot towards McCauley's black car. As the pick-up draws alongside, McCauley tells the driver to keep his hands in sight and to throw the package in through the car window with one hand. Unseen by McCauley, a gunman slips down from the pick-up's rear and creeps up on him. Shiherlis, on a nearby rooftop, spots him and warns McCauley through

Shiherlis asleep (top); McCauley admonishes Charlene (below)

his headset. McCauley slams into reverse, crushing the gunman. Shiherlis then riddles the pick-up with shots from his automatic rifle. The pick-up speeds away, deserting the injured gunman, who is caught in the crossfire and then rammed by McCauley. As the pick-up comes by Cheritto, waiting at the entrance, fires several shotgun blasts, killing the driver. The package is waste paper. McCauley calls Van Zant from a restaurant kitchen phone to tell him to 'keep the money'. 'I don't understand,' says Van Zant. 'I'm talking to an empty telephone,' says McCauley, 'because there's a dead man on the other end of this fucking line.'

We're back here to where the film feels most itself, in choreographed gunplay and sharp macho dialogue, with De Niro incarnating the avenging nemesis he's played in so many other films. No one delivers that kind of threat with as much menace as De Niro. We feel the kick of genre as we get back to visceral pleasures and away from complex domestic angst.

Shiherlis peppers the pickup (top); 'I'm talking to an empty telephone' (below)

5 Drinking in the Dark

The sadness of domestic conflict, tentative love and dysfunctional work-home arrangements persists, even though we now slip into a series of apparent celebrations. Alongside the pleasure-seeking, the discreet politics of *Heat* begins to bite deeper; the class and status of certain characters are set in powerful contrast to the wealthy norm. And though the domestic scenes are mostly behind us, the differences between the men and women will be brought into jagged relief by a confrontation between Justine and Hanna, which is the counterpart to McCauley meeting Eady and serves as the moment when the film starts to leave the women behind. It's a portrait of a relationship in decline to match the other's first flush of possibility.

But before we look at that I want to focus on one of the most awkward yet touching subplots of *Heat*: the story of Donald Breedan (Dennis Haysbert – best known for playing the presidential candidate in the TV series *24*). Breedan is an African American man just out of Folsom, starting his first day's work at a diner as a grill man. Encouraged by his wife/lover (we never find out which) he turns up. But the diner's manager demands a 25 per cent kickback in return for good reports to the parole officer. Reluctantly Breedan buckles down to the drudgery, but a few scenes later, his wife/lover finds him despairingly drunk in a bar. She tells him she's proud of him. This scene is a strange transposition of

Breedan takes a drink

a scene from *L.A. Takedown* in which Hanna's wife says the same of him after he's complained that 'today I made no difference'. Breedan's role in *L.A. Takedown* is merely to turn up unexplained as the getaway driver at the climactic bank robbery. In *Heat* we see him as a victim, trapped by the US legal system into a criminal life he'd clearly like to break free from, though his fate is likewise to be at the wheel for the crew. His place in the cop–criminal hierarchy is as one of the working class. Unlike the two other prominent African American men in the film – Albert Torena, the sharply dressed snitch, and the upstanding Sergeant Drucker, a white-collar conservative, Breedan dresses in the sweatshirt and jeans of a guy who's expected to 'clean up and haul out the trash' before he can take a break. In these next few scenes, while glasses are raised to lips, Los Angeles changes from Shiherlis's playground of 'risk versus reward' to something more like Breedan's dark city of confinement and surveillance.

When McCauley's men and their wives get together at a restaurant for Elaine's birthday, they are as smartly dressed as any other L.A. success stories. To the casual eye there is barely a whiff of Folsom about them. They're ostensibly just middle-class business people enjoying the plentiful spoils of their labour. And since, by repute, L.A.'s smart spots might exclude anyone who wasn't dressed that way, their appearance is both aspirational display and necessary disguise.

    McCauley, though, is feeling out of it and perhaps jealous of his companions. He calls Eady and asks to see her. She tells him to come on over. On leaving the restaurant, the crew is being watched by Hanna and his officers from the roof opposite. Tipped off with Michael Cheritto's name by Albert Torena's brother, who heard him using the term 'slick', the police have bugged his home phones and vehicles and got on to Shiherlis's and Trejo's too. Only McCauley is as yet unknown to them, but he will now be followed. Then comes one of the few false moments in *Heat*. When the crew has gone, Hanna and his men emerge from their hiding place, behind a neon sign. They all stand up in a row and Hanna says (with little conviction) 'When these guys come out of whatever score

Cheritto, Elaine and Anna at Elaine's birthday dinner

'You a regular rodeo rider'

they are going to pull down next, they are going to get the surprise of their fucking lives.'

But his prediction does lace the next scene with irony. Lying on a bed in a motel room and baring his tattooed bulk is *Heat*'s other prominent member of the working class – Waingro. A young black prostitute is praising his performance as she dresses to return to the street: 'You a regular rodeo rider. This was the monster fuck of my young life,' she says. Waingro looks at her piercingly, in a way that reminds us of De Niro, playing the equally tattooed Max Cady in Scorsese's version of *Cape Fear* (1991). Waingro tells her, 'You don't have a truth-telling way about you. You don't know what this is, do you? The grim reaper is visiting with you.' As Waingro grabs her hair, the film cuts to a bottle-top being yanked off. The beer is for Waingro, now sitting in a bar, hustling for work.

It's a truly shocking moment; a reminder of what random violence is really about. Given its keen interest in domestic lives, *Heat* is not a particularly violent crime film. But Mann is expert at making such moments count. He often juxtaposes murderousness with aspects of tenderness and intimacy. Holding a blade to the throat of the heroine

Cora in *The Last of the Mohicans*, an Iroquois brave seems to be almost caressing her. Towards the end of *Heat*, Cheritto picks up a young girl in harm's way with some gentleness, only to use her as a human shield. The prostitute's murder is made all the more appalling by the combination of visual metaphor (the bottle top being wrenched off at the moment we expect to see her neck being broken) and the reticence that keeps the act itself off screen. It's a killing of much greater importance than those generic, distanced deaths of the shot-up guards or of Van Zant's wiped-out heavies.

Kevin Gage plays Waingro as a cartoon psychopath: an incarnation of evil that has to be extreme to make us love McCauley by contrast. (The Max Cady connection may well be intended to make him McCauley's alter ego through the casting of De Niro.) The film's lack of empathy for Waingro, this unknowable force – a serial killer on the side – counterbalances the excess of empathy towards McCauley, whose own morality is at least as sociopathic, if more logical. The irony is that Waingro is the one who really lives his life by McCauley's code, who disposes of domestic attachments with brutality, who has no need to disguise his malignancy on the streets. Waingro exists by pure will. He is a knowing agent of fate, and McCauley's true nemesis. Killing the girl is his idea of a celebration and he caps it by visiting that most working class of haunts: a bar.

Cora caressed in *The Last of the Mohicans* (Twentieth Century Fox Film Corporation, 1992)

Once Hanna's team have 'made' McCauley's crew, we know by the rules of genre that we are on the downward slope towards the eventual killing or capture of the villains. *Heat* is no different in this respect, except that the descent is much longer, less steep and more involved than in most crime films. From here forward we will see less and less of the women until near the end, as their significance ebbs in favour of thriller dynamics. But here also comes their testament in the scene that pits Justine's idea of a shared life against Hanna's own commandments – his version of thou shalt have no commitments.

The detectives are having their own night out with their wives when Hanna gets paged to a crime scene and has to leave Justine at the table. The prostitute has been found. He is examining the body when he has to stop the dead girl's mother approaching, which he does by

'I guess the earth shattered?'

embracing her. There is something uncomfortable about this white authority figure hugging this impoverished, grieving black woman (hugging African Americans is something Pacino also does a lot in his next film, *City Hall*, 1997). It seems like a hollow justification for his role. Hanna is playing at nurturing – something he doesn't do for real at home. By the time Hanna returns to the restaurant, Justine is still there, alone and sick of being shut out of his working life.

JUSTINE: I guess the earth shattered.
HANNA: So why didn't you let Bosko take you home?
JUSTINE: I didn't want to ruin his night too. What was it?
HANNA: You don't want to know.
JUSTINE: I'd like to know what's behind that grim look on your face.

HANNA: Now I don't do that. You know it. Let's go.

JUSTINE: You never told me I'd be excluded.

HANNA: I told you when we hooked up baby that you were going to have to share me with all the bad people and all the ugly events on this planet.

JUSTINE: And I bought into that *sharing* because I love you. I love you fat, bald, young, old, money, no money, driving a bus – I don't care, but you have got to be present like a normal guy some of the time. That's sharing. This isn't sharing, this is leftovers.

HANNA: I see. What I should do is come home and say, hi honey, guess what, I walked into this house today where this junkie asshole just fried his baby in a microwave because it was crying too loud, so let me share that with you. C'mon, let's share that and in sharing it we'll somehow cathartically dispel all that heinous shit, right? Wrong. You know why?

JUSTINE: Because you prefer the normal routine: we fuck and you lose the power of speech.

HANNA: Because I've got to hold onto my angst, I preserve it because I need it. It keeps me sharp, on the edge, where I've got to be.

JUSTINE: You don't live with me. You live with the remains of dead people. You sift through the detritus; you read the terrain; you search for signs of passing, for the scent of your prey, and then you hunt them down. That's the only thing you're committed to. The rest is the mess you leave as you pass through. What I don't understand is why I can't cut loose of you.

This is hardly regular crime film 'husband and wife stuff'. What kind of restaurant row about relationships gets into such language as 'detritus' or 'signs of passing'? What makes it even more curious is that Justine's words seem to be partly inspired by a few words said to Al Pacino by Ellen Barkin in Harold Becker's *Sea of Love* (1989), where he plays a cop and she his lover. Barkin's character has told the cop she always feels safe in her neighbourhood so he's told her about three murders that have occurred there in the past year. She says, 'This town is like one big city of the dead for you, huh?' Pacino's response, however, is the opposite of the one he gives as Hanna. 'City of the dead, what'd you say that for? I love life. I'm just trying to share with you, you know. When you live with

Ellen Barkin and Pacino
in *Sea of Love* (Universal
Pictures, 1989)

a cop there are certain things, cop's eyes, what we see. You know. There's
you, what you see, which is like nuthin', and there's our eyes, our life,
what we see.'

But Hanna's eyes see farther than this cop's, as the dream he will
later relate to McCauley will show, and Los Angeles really is one big city of
the dead for him. Both men 'perceive the world with a peculiar clarity,'
says Mann, 'and are driven very intensely from inside themselves. Their
preciseness is a way of telling whoever they're talking to that they're
simple, yet profound: "Listen to each word I am telling you," they're
saying. "I don't have time to fuck around with a lot of adjectives and
adverbs."'[26]

As fans who repeatedly quote from *GoodFellas* (1990) and *Pulp
Fiction* (1994) remind us, highly unrealistic modes of dialogue are one of
Hollywood's key pleasures. We don't hesitate to enjoy McCauley's reply
to Van Zant – 'because there's a dead man on the other end of this
fucking line' (which is lifted from *The Jericho Mile*) – because there's a
tradition for that kind of macho grandstanding. Yet there is no real
equivalent in the New Hollywood action movie for talk between male
and female adults, or at least nothing much beyond the flip humour of,
say, George Clooney and Jennifer Lopez in the car trunk in *Out of Sight*
(1998).

It's a symptom of the oppositions that Mann likes to set up that
these men who have no time for adjectives and adverbs are regularly

confronted by smart women who in turn seem, by some of their phraseology – 'not making forward progress', 'maintain a consistent mood' – to have read a lot of self-help books. Their language has a parroted quality that goes against the smooth grain of the men's crime-speak (although they too are capable of the exaggerated line – take McCauley's line to Eady, 'I'm a needle going back to zero, a double blank'). The contrast is effective in setting up the usual notion that the sexes speak different languages, but weak in the sense of restricting the scenes with women to a therapeutic ghetto of sensitivity and inaction. Despite these restrictions the terrific performances of Ashley Judd and Diane Venora somehow make these book speeches into forceful, full-blooded challenges of injured dignity.

Justine's condemnation of Hanna illustrates the difficulty Mann has with tone every time he reaches out of genre for a sense of a higher form. He seems desperate to grant some profundity to Justine while keeping her within a generic structure that usually excludes women from bearing too much meaning. He has to work hard with her role because Hanna needs to be challenged by her, and so she gets these lines which no one could make sound natural. But where in *L.A. Takedown*, portentous dialogue can be cringeworthy, here it works because Venora and Pacino are such a great pairing. However awkwardly, Mann is here trying to forge a new hybrid of melodrama, tragedy and thriller. I admire his chutzpah, and it's part of the thrill of the film to experience the partial profundities and the near-nonsense running together.

We now know what kind of unconditional love Hanna is giving up with Justine: one that simply requires him to sometimes be around and say something. He can't even manage that. His detectives have had their night out. Breedan has nursed his whiskey and McCauley, in a brief scene, has persuaded Eady to run away to New Zealand with him soon. But all of these moments of R&R look, in this supremely workaholic film, like mere pit stops, 'lube jobs' as Hanna's wife in *L.A. Takedown* has it. Only Waingro seems to have profoundly enjoyed himself.

6 Face to Face

Thieves in the night, 'on the prowl' as Hanna puts it. *Heat* is about to re-
enter the semi-religious quietude of the procedural crime thriller
humming along contentedly. The viewer's senses are put on alert by the
sense of anticipation as the crew make ready to break into the Precious
Metals Depository – a job they already had planned before the Kelso and
Van Zant scams were suggested. *Heat* keeps us sharp by the surprise and
subtlety with which it assaults our eyes and more especially, here, our
ears.

Music is so well integrated into the film's texture it seems like a
constant presence, one unending orchestrated swelling and receding of
semi-industrial noises. Yet the score is actually a segue of selected tracks,
tied together by incidental pieces from the composer Elliot Goldenthal.
They all have a minimalist portentousness about them that suits the high-
tech gloss of *Heat*, from the Kronos Quartet's drones to Terje Rypdal's
guitar to Moby's raging synthscapes. Mann's willingness to cross-
orchestrate between this music and his diegetic event sound, each
commenting on the other, brings a fresh understanding to the meaning
of a film soundscape. But there's also a plentiful use of silence, as the
scene of the robbery will demonstrate.

Mann had originally wanted to use the music of Glenn Branca's
massed guitar orchestra, but changed his mind. What's interesting about
the Branca connection is that his breakthrough as a composer was in
1979–80, around the time of the first draft of *Heat*. For me much of the
aesthetic of the film reaches back to that moment. *Heat* seems a
repository for many cultural and subcultural aspects of the 1980s and
90s. Vestiges of what we now think of as 1980s style – the big fascistic
corporate buildings, the posturing in exaggerated suits, the obsession
with work and with designer-label consumer goods – are pervasive
here.[27] I will deal with 1980s 'style' later, but what makes this haunting
of *Heat* by the previous decade seem all the more apt is the casting of De
Niro and Pacino, actors whose iconic status was secure in the 1980s but
for whom the early 1990s proved a sticky period of transition.

McCauley is about to become aware the LAPD is watching him, and this section of *Heat* ends with the famous coffee-house meeting between him and Hanna. Before we cover these events, though, I want to consider what De Niro and Pacino bring to the film's table. Their reputations as the finest actors of their generation were both cemented by the same film – Coppola's *The Godfather Part II* (1974) – though they were never on screen together. Pacino reprised his role as Michael Corleone, and De Niro played his father Vito as a poor young man in flashbacks, linking both of them to American cinema's most iconic post-war actor, Marlon Brando, who played the ageing Vito. *Heat* was therefore unique in bringing the two together on screen. That's what allowed this expensive crime thriller to get made. As Mann tells it, it all fell together very rapidly. 'Art Linson [*Heat*'s producer] was going to be spending Christmas with Bob, and we thought, "Yes, let's pursue Bob." He gave the script to Bob, he liked it and said, simply, "Yes, let's do it." In the meantime, I gave the script to Al, and he said, "Yeah".'[28] Casting the rest of the roles then became easy.

If *Heat* is, as I suggest, a timely meeting place for a number of zeitgeist concerns, the project is fortunate to have captured both lead actors at the pinnacle of their careers. By this I mean a number of things:

- *Heat* captured performances that are definitive of the two actors' 'middle-aged' personas as stars and actors.
- Their roles in *Heat* distil elements of other roles they have played throughout their careers, and not just in the sense of the iconic weight their screen presence and familiarity brings to every role. (In other words, their personas are deliberately manipulated.)
- *Heat* caught them both at a moment when they could still play men of keen physical instincts. (The imminence of ageing adds pathos to Hanna and McCauley's attempts to cling to their street personas.)

Pacino's movie persona has been slowly etched onto a face that gives direct access to a character's essence. His challenging brown eyes are

sometimes windows, sometimes opaque. In *The Godfather* (1972), even
at his most deceitful (when having lunch with enemies he's about to blow
away) or most glacial (when he's about to abandon his brother Freddo)
you can read his thought processes when he wants you to. By the time he
made *Sea of Love*, Pacino's mid-life self was a bundle of carefully
directed intensities in a comfortably compact frame. Clothes draped off
him with a semi-sloppy elegance. His mannerisms had an off-the-cuff
savoir faire an inch away from showmanship. *Sea of Love* was his third
major cop role: in *Serpico* (1973), he's the archetypal groovy undercover
cop who breaks all the rules and in *Cruising* (1980) he hunts a killer in
New York's S&M gay scene. *Sea of Love* seemed to kick off a new spate
of creativity. The cop's bumbling charm and lightly worn melancholy
were further adapted in the roles leading up to *Heat*. *Frankie and Johnny*
(1991), *Glengarry Glen Ross* (1992), *Scent of a Woman* (1992) and
Carlito's Way (1993) all feel to me like unwitting preparation for *Heat*.
Pacino's armoury of techniques is formidable, but it doesn't disguise the
fresh persona that coalesced around the actor between 1989 and 1993.
That persona's definitive form is Vincent Hanna.

Hanna is a much slicker, more intuitive and energetic cop than *Sea
of Love*'s Frank Keller, though, as we have seen, he is similarly aware of
death. His way with women is less needy than the short-order cook
Pacino played opposite Michelle Pfeiffer in *Frankie and Johnny*, yet he
carries a similar sense of weary romance. The aggression of Pacino's
salesman in *Glengarry Glen Ross* is ever-present in Hanna, amplified by
the talent for sudden bellowing seen in *Scent of a Woman*. Carlito's
prowling and commanding of the streets with pure gesture also carry
straight into the Homicide Lieutenant. It's the absolute commitment
when Pacino performs, the feeling that nothing is held back, that makes
Hanna such a vivid incarnation.

In the early 1990s De Niro was beginning to get a reputation for
coasting. The full-on intensity of his 1970s performances was missing
from such late-80s parts as the shy lover in *Stanley & Iris* (1989), or the
convict on the run in *We're No Angels* (1989). He seemed to be trying to
stretch his range into areas where he could not be typecast. The physical

skill required for the catatonic Parkinson's victim in *Awakenings* (1990), and his menacing turn as a conscience-free mafia hood in *GoodFellas*, brought him back into focus. But then his flat portrayal of a 1950s film director called to rat out his friends to the House Un-American Activities Committee in *Guilty By Suspicion* (1990), his impassive fireman in *Backdraft* (1991), and an anonymous cameo in *Mistress* (1991) put the blur back on him.

Given the redundant task of reprising one of Robert Mitchum's great roles as the sadistic killer Max Cady in Scorsese's remake of *Cape Fear*, De Niro pushed the role into big bad wolf parody, creating a crazed fanatic whose body is covered in tattooed apocalyptic warnings of vengeance. His sweet turn in *Mad Dog and Glory* (1992) as a shy cop who gets the mobster's girl, showed a measured light touch; whereas his nervy street hustler in *Night and the City* (1992) was another evaporating display, and his supporting role as a bus driver in his directing debut *A Bronx Tale* (1993) made him a quiet authority figure of some force. If the De Niro of the 1990s seemed less sparky than before, he was also taking bigger risks. You can even suspect a slickness about his Sam 'Ace' Rothstein, the mob gambler he played in Scorsese's *Casino* (1995). However, Rothstein is a man who lets the irrelevances of life slide off him – not usually a De Niro character trait – so, in acting terms, the easiness fits. Sometimes De Niro is too subtle to be De Niro.

So the actor came to *Heat* after his card pack of characters had been shuffled to random. He was no longer the cool Bobby of the 1970s for whom every role was a hipster triumph. Instead he was a much quieter figure, a steady Hollywood choice for characters on the inside with an outsider's intensity. With the fiery Pacino opposite him, he took Neil McCauley to be a cautious man of great self-control, whose simmering anger is damped down tight. His aggressive sense of will is similar to his hood from *GoodFellas*, he has some of the shyness of the cop from *Mad Dog and Glory*, and his command of the screen echoes the bus driver in *A Bronx Tale*. McCauley embodies all that we want from a mid-term De Niro. We get his genius at threatening behaviour but we also get his more recent ability to fix our attention without doing much.

In *Heat* both the co-stars seem to be the essence of who we think they are.

A small string section plays single sustained notes as a helicopter shot swoops down from a view of Downtown's skyscrapers to pick out a black van heading into an industrial area. Awaiting its imminent arrival, LAPD Homicide officers and SWAT troops are in hiding around the Precious Metals Depository. Hanna and his closest associates are in the back of a truck parked among several others across the street. They see the van arrive at the door on their two monitors, one a normal black-and-white set, the other from a night vision camera that gives an image in negative.

Tension mounts among the watchers as the crew gets out. Cheritto climbs a telegraph pole and Shiherlis prepares the lock tools. Hanna watches with terse appreciation: 'technique', he says as Cheritto switches off the alarm systems using a tapped-in laptop, 'open-sesame, right there' as the lock is broken. The music changes intervals but remains low in volume, so one can hear the dripping of water from a leak hitting the floor as McCauley and Shiherlis enter the building. While Shiherlis begins drilling the safes, McCauley goes back outside to keep watch, receding into the shadows of a corner near the door (rather like Orson Welles's Harry Lime in *The Third Man*, 1949). He can only now be seen on the night vision monitor. Sound levels jump from the quiet strings to the loud screaming of the drill and back again.

Inside Hanna's truck, a doltish SWAT trooper sits down clumsily, clattering his rifle against the side of the truck. McCauley hears the noise and turns to stone. The strings are playing very high notes. McCauley stares out into the darkness directly at the truck. His face, listening, and Hanna's, watching, alternate on screen as the music climbs even higher, note by note. We are reminded of Will Graham's sixth sense in *Manhunter*. It's a pivotal moment, because for the first time Hanna and McCauley have each sniffed the other out. 'He's heard, he's heard,' whispers Bosko, as McCauley walks into the building and tells Shiherlis they must walk away, now. The SWAT team captain wants to rush them but Hanna orders him to let the crew go. He doesn't want them caught

Hanna and his team wait

Shiherlis uses the drill

on a misdemeanour charge that will see them on the streets again in
mere months.

That image of McCauley in negative on the monitor makes him a
ghost, the counterpart to Hanna's earlier resemblance to a night
creature. Surveillance brings them together, as if it's only the sensitivities
of special equipment that can spot these special people. But surveillance
is also the way Mann sets up a series of teases heightening Hanna and
McCauley's interest in one another, leading up to the famous coffee-
house confrontation that was both the origin of the film and its major
selling point.

One of the most nicely observed of *Heat*'s scenes comes next.
McCauley and his crew gather together in a deserted spot to decide what to
do now they know they're being watched. You can see that the younger
actors revere De Niro and are happy to play it quiet and pay attention.
McCauley seems to have become fatalistically calm, his chin pressing
inwards to his chest with caution. He tells them, 'Our problem is, take the
bank or split right now – do not go home, do not pack, nuthin'. Thirty
seconds from now we are gone on our separate ways, that's it.' He looks at
Shiherlis, grim with tension, who says, 'The bank is worth the risk. I need it

brother.' When a nervous Michael Cheritto seeks assurances, McCauley tells him. 'I got plans, I'm going away after this, so for me maybe the reward is worth the stretch.' He reminds Cheritto about his family and all the money he's got stashed away, 'If I were you I would be smart, I would stay clear of this.' But Cheritto gives his answer, 'Well, for me, you know, the action *is* the juice.' They're all in.

Though De Niro scrupulously avoids here the pantomime exaggeration of his roles in *Cape Fear* and *Mary Shelley's Frankenstein* (1994), Pacino gives unashamed vent to burlesque interrogations, and he is terrific. When surveillance on Charlene's phone leads the cops straight to her lover, Alan Marciano (Han Azaria), in Las Vegas, Hanna and Drucker storm into his office. He protests their lack of jurisdiction. They introduce him to a Vegas officer who has an old, New Jersey warrant for Marciano's arrest on cigarette smuggling charges. Hanna's idea is that Marciano will persuade Charlene to turn against Chris. 'Why did I ever get mixed up with that bitch?' Marciano says. A nettled Hanna roars, 'BECAUSE SHE'S GOT A GREAT ASS. AND YOU'VE GOT YOUR HEAD ALL THE WAY UP IT!' Then, as if in self-appreciation, he adds, 'Ferocious, ain't I?'

This is good showmanship, but there's a much better earlier example, which happens straight after Hanna has rowed with Justine over the burnt dinner, when he visits his snitch, Albert Torena. Pacino and Sergeant Drucker find him at a car chop-shop down a dirt road, just as he's sitting down to breakfast. This is a throwback to similar meetings in *Starsky and Hutch* between the two detectives and the pimp Huggy

Bear. The genre trope demands that the snitch must be coerced into giving up information he knows he will have to give up anyway.

'Oh man this ain't Disneyland,' says the pretty boy Torena. 'Why haven't you answered my calls?' asks Hanna, sweeping the cutlery from the table as he sits down to stare, an inch from his victim. As Torena starts stuttering excuses, Hanna shouts, 'I do for you, but you don't do for me.' When Torena's spiel about being up all night stutters to a halt, Drucker says, 'Let's violate his ass right now.' The talk overlaps because Hanna isn't listening. 'Tell us you fell in love,' he says, 'I'll buy that.' Torena says he's like a dancer retrieving information, but Hanna roars, 'GIVE ME ALL YOU GOT. GIVE ME ALL YOU GOT.' He's at the edge of any kind of plausibility as a real cop. 'I got something for you, man,' Torena

'Take the bank or split right now?'

Ferocious Hanna

'They're looking at us, the LAPD'

says at last. 'It's my brother.' 'Your brother?' Hanna asks, and looks under the table. 'Is he here?' 'No man, he in Phoenix.' Hanna starts singing, 'By the time I get to Phoenix, she'll be rising ...'

Pacino's routine with Ricky Harris is pure pleasure, not funny *per se*, but a wonderful piece of acting on all sides. Such ferocity and farce pours from the small frame of Pacino you would think he was a stand-up comedian. At one remove the dialogue is ridiculous, a pure riff on the most traditional of crime confrontations, and yet it works as a genuinely dramatic confontation. *Heat* features a lot of talk that seems to simply fuel our fascination in character from one stage to the next, rather than to deepen the suspense. The drama comes as much from the counterpoint between Hanna's scenes and McCauley's. For at the same time that Hanna is stoking up this malevolent ringmaster persona – an act within an act – McCauley goes deeper into himself.

After Hanna's coercion of Marciano, the crew is at a dockyard container facility, in sunshine, scoping out the next job (this is one time when they behave like the cops, with that public sense of ownership). When they drive off, the cops come down from their hiding places to figure out the crew's plan. Nothing makes sense, and Hanna is perplexed until he realises what's going on. Three times he says to his men, 'You want to know what they're looking at?' as if he was in a David Mamet play. 'I mean is this guy something or what?' His admiration is to the fore now. 'They're looking at us, the LAPD. We've been made.' Hanna parades around in the sunshine, posing, gesturing and looking upwards, as if he were a model at a fashion shoot, knowing McCauley is there with his camera. Again the super-sensory connection has been made.

Nate tells McCauley later that Hanna is a 'real hot-dog', with a 'hard-on' for guys like him, advising him to take a pass and disappear. McCauley reiterates that it's worth the risk, knowing this is his one chance to make a clean break with Eady. Hanna, meanwhile, finds Justine getting ready to go out without him. He decides to go back to work.

Now we see the 'City of Lights' laid out below us again as Hanna's chopper negotiates the towers of Downtown before heading out to the LAX airport freeway, where McCauley is currently being tailed by Hanna's men.

Commandeering one of the tailing cars, he speeds to catch up with McCauley. It's one of those glossy sequences that Mann does so well of vehicles and lights speeding through the night city, while Moby's 'New Dawn Fades' energises the soundtrack. Putting on his flashing cop lights to get McCauley to pull over, Hanna gingerly approaches his car. 'What do you say I buy you a cup of coffee?' Hanna offers. McCauley, though perplexed, agrees.

Though the coffee-house scene is the first in which Pacino and De Niro have ever acted together, at no time do we see both their faces. This gave rise to the accusation that the two were somehow shot separately. Production stills showing both together, in situ, refute this. The scene was shot simply, using telephoto lenses at a distance, and at a slight angle away from head on.

Michael Mann's script notes for this scene were published in *Sight and Sound*, and they give an insight to Mann's orchestration of the emotions to any scene. The script was dated 22 June 1996 and the notes are mostly in green ink with red felt-pen additions and emphases. For instance, this is the note about Hanna's motivation for setting up the meeting: 'BACK STORY – You left the dysfunctional marital arena for the engaging dynamic complex one, as if simmering in the subconscious was dilemma: a surveillance of a man cognizant of it: go meet him, go get him, talk to him.' How lightly this note sidelines Hanna's fall-out with Justine, as if it's nothing much, merely the inspiration for an audacious move. Mann's notes for McCauley are more about his curiosity: 'DIR. Neil [thinking]: Is this guy nuts? What is this about? What's goin' on? No other units … Yeah, I'll talk to him. He wants to find out about me? I'll find out about him.'

The conversation opens with some polite chit-chat about prisons. McCauley is open about his record but Hanna starts gently digging:

HANNA: McNeil as tough as they say?

MCCAULEY: You looking to become a penologist?

HANNA: You lookin' to go back? I chased down some crews, guys just lookin' to fuck-up, get busted back. That you?

MCCAULEY: You must have worked some dipshit crews.

HANNA: I worked all kinds.

'That's the discipline'

'That's pretty vacant'

MCCAULEY: You see me doing thrill-seeker liquor store holdups with a 'Born to
   Lose' tattoo on my chest?
HANNA: No, I do not.
MCCAULEY: Right. And I am never going back.

At this point the script says: 'the adversarial intensity is eye-to-eye'.
One brilliant effect of the two actors being shot in exactly the same way
but never together is to convey the idea that each is looking into a mirror
(with all its echoes of De Niro's roles in *Taxi Driver*, 1976, and *Raging
Bull*, 1980). Ostensibly this scene is pedestrian – talking heads yo-yoing
back and forth – but already the tantalising of our expectations has
worked. De Niro and Pacino are both masters of conversational intensity,
and even within the parameters of the inward-looking McCauley, De
Niro's insistence that he is 'never going back' is still laced with threat.

HANNA: Then don't take down scores.
MCCAULEY: I do what I do best. I take scores. You do what you do best: trying
   to stop guys like me.
HANNA: You never wanted a regular type life?

MCCAULEY: What the fuck is that? Barbecues and ballgames?

HANNA: Yeah.

MCCAULEY: This regular-type life. That your life?

HANNA: No. My life is a disaster zone. I got a step-daughter who's fucked up because her real father's this large type asshole. My wife and I are passing each other on the downslope of our marriage, my third, 'cause every moment I got I spend chasing guys like you around the block.

MCCAULEY: A guy told me one time, don't let yourself get attached to anything you're not willing to walk out on, if you feel the heat coming round the corner, in 30 seconds flat. So if you are on me and you gotta move when I move, how do you expect to keep a marriage?

HANNA: What are you, a monk?

MCCAULEY: No. I got a woman.

HANNA: What do you tell her?

MCCAULEY: She thinks I'm a salesman.

HANNA: And if you spot me around the corner … You gonna walk out? Not say goodbye?

MCCAULEY: That's the discipline.

HANNA: That's pretty vacant.

MCCAULEY: Yeah? It is what it is. That or do something else.

HANNA: I don't know how to do anything else.

MCCAULEY: Neither do I.

HANNA: And I don't much want to.

MCCAULEY: … neither do I.

McCauley and Hanna are explaining the psychology of the film to each other, making sure we know that there is more to these guys than the desire to do battle. They start out edgy, with each trying to slyly draw the other out. To their mutual surprise, they become intimate and bring us back to considering their incompatibility with domestic life. It's the film's way of saying, enough of the talk, time now for action. Confirmation that we are heading in the direction of death comes from the dream that Hanna now relates:

HANNA: I'm at this big banquet table and all the victims of all the murders I've worked are there. They're looking at me with black eyeballs 'cause they got eightball hemorrhages from head shot wounds. Big bloated balloon people 'cause I found 'em after two weeks under the bed when the neighbors reported the smell. They're all there.

MCCAULEY: What do they say?

HANNA: Nothing.

MCCAULEY: There's no talk?

HANNA: No. They don't have anything to say. We look at each other. They look at me. That's the dream.

MCCAULEY: I have one where I'm drowning. And I gotta wake myself up and start breathing or I'll die in my sleep.

HANNA: You know what that's about?

MCCAULEY: Yeah. Having enough time.

HANNA: Time enough to do what you want to do?

MCCAULEY: That's right.

HANNA: You doing it now?

MCCAULEY: No. Not yet.

They recognise their kinship. It amuses and touches them. There's only time left now for threats and warnings. Each issues one that is a duplicate of the other. The gist is that they like each other but if either one has got to shoot the other in the course of action, they 'will not hesitate'. Though Hanna feels he is about to close McCauley down, McCauley is equally sure he can shake off the cops. The sense of fate closing in is all the more important here because the film is about to break out from its claustrophobic mode in which these two protagonists behave like people confined by others' expectations. For the gunfight, which follows the bank job, is like a sudden eruption into the great outdoors, the moment when these men of action shake off their brooding on the messiness of their lives and seemingly incarnate their perfected selves.

7 Concrete Canyons

Returning from meeting McCauley, Hanna is told that the traces on the crew have been dumped. None of his men now knows their whereabouts. They are in fact breaking into electronic circuits that will allow them to control the Far East National Bank's alarm systems. We cut to Van Zant's office, which he has not left since McCauley pronounced him dead. Waingro has come to offer his services. Having told Van Zant that McCauley is 'real thorough', he promises, 'I can make some moves here.'

'I can make some moves here'

And then we're in the diner where Breedan works. McCauley, Shiherlis and Cheritto have gathered for the pre-heist meet. Again they're all in Samurai mode, getting tetchy about the absence of Trejo when he calls, saying he has cops all over him, 'like a cheap suit'. McCauley, though, has already seen Breedan behind the counter and remembered him from Folsom D-wing. He offers him the job of driver, 'Right here, right now.' Breedan considers it for several seconds before

'Right here, right now'

agreeing, taking the opportunity to shove his boss to the floor on his way out.

I doubt there's a more formidable and exciting action sequence in any other film than what follows. There has been no music during snatched scenes of Eady and Charlene at their homes. Then the electro-percussive pulse of Eno's 'Force Marker' kicks in like adrenaline. Its cross-rhythms maintain a constant tension during the proceedings.

McCauley saunters into the bank, like an echo of Hanna's crime scene entrance, with the suggestion of a swagger. He's dressed in his black pin-stripe suit, and has a small earpiece with a black lead in his right ear. Cheritto and Shiherlis come in after him, each in grey suits with similar earpieces – only Cheritto is obviously carrying something weapon-like under his jacket – if you look closely. They're not looking that discreet, just invisible enough.

At a given moment McCauley and Cheritto pull on black balaclavas with eye-slits and take out their sub-machine-guns. Shiherlis saps a security guard viciously, without warning (before putting on his own balaclava) while Cheritto does the same to another. McCauley orders a third, at gunpoint, to get on his knees and put his hands behind his back for tying. He then kicks the guard onto his face. Cherrito is now busy warning people to stay down. Climbing onto the counter, McCauley warns everyone to get on the floor and keep their hands on their heads.

McCauley enters the bank

When the bank manager denies knowledge of the vault keys, McCauley punches him, rips the keys from his neck, and tells him to 'sit there and let it bleed'. Shiherlis enters the vault and fills three holdalls with cash.

The way the scene is so crisply edited encourages us to sit back and appreciate the sheer efficiency of this heist – the fact that the three cloth holdalls Shiherlis has in his briefcase each fit the huge packed cash bundles perfectly seems audacious. The way that McCauley controls the heist from the top of the counter, and warns people that it is not their money that's being stolen, has a touch of *Bonnie and Clyde* (1967). It also seems a little reminiscent of the Dead Presidents' bank raids in Kathryn Bigelow's *Point Break* (1991), performed by surfers in plastic masks. There's none of the bloody amateurism associated with *Reservoir Dogs* and *Killing Zoe* (1994).

Just as the heist seems successfully complete, Robbery–Homicide receives a tip-off from Van Zant's man Hugh Benny (Henry Rollins), giving the bank's location and the time. Hanna and his men are on their way in what seems like no time.

With one holdall each, the crew exits the bank. Cheritto goes first, smoothing his hair and putting on shades, quickly reaching Breedan in the car, where he begins to celebrate. McCauley and Shiherlis come out together, sharp and aware and also in shades, but their walk seems to take an eternity. Mann's manipulation of time here is extraordinary, lengthening the walk while the cops arrive speedily and disperse, ready to take them down. Hanna orders them to wait until the thieves are in the car, 'clean shots and watch your background'. Roadblocks are in place. Casals (Wes Studi) and Drucker, concealed by a moving tourist coach, are trying to outflank the car. Hanna and Bosko are moving down the pavement, warning bystanders to get out of the way, ducking behind cover.

McCauley gets into the car. Shiherlis is about to join him when he spots Drucker. Without hestitation he opens fire with his sub-machine-gun and the noise is quite unlike anything ever heard in the movies before. 'We went to great pains,' said Mann, 'to be sure we got the right sound for the machine guns letting rip in the concrete canyons. There's a certain pattern to the reverberation. It makes you think you've never heard that in a film before, so it feels very real and authentic. Then you really believe the jeopardy these people are in.'[29]

Heat now becomes more like a war film or a Western than a crime saga. Everyone is armed with heavy weaponry, and the sound is astonishing in its variety of penetrations and ricochets. Shiherlis shoots Bosko dead and then gets in the car, which speeds off towards the police roadblock only to be peppered with gunfire. Casals blows the tyres with a shotgun blast, Breedan is killed, and the car collides into a row of stationary vehicles. The three surviving crew members evacuate.

And now, while Cherrito attacks wide of them, McCauley and Shiherlis become iconic action men. Acting as a two-man assault team, they each giving covering fire while the other runs. This scene may be Val Kilmer's finest hour in the cinema. He has never looked so at ease as he is here, blazing away with a sub-machine-gun.

Shiherlis and McCauley, a two-man assault team

Robert Longo, *Untitled, 1981* (courtesy the artist and Metro Pictures)

The gunfight is set in the heart of Downtown, and these men in suits, framed by the fascistic steel and glass towers behind them, seem to be symbols of rampant self-interest. McCauley is now a powerhouse in shades. The images are reminiscent of Robert Longo's 1979–82 high-contrast black-and-white series of figure drawings and relief friezes of buildings, *Men in the Cities*, another factor anchoring the film back to the time of the script's inception.

Many of the roadblock police are shot, but despite the dozens of weapons firing at them, McCauley and Shiherlis seem impossible to hit. Hanna is running to catch up. McCauley wounds officer Schwartz (Jerry Trimble), but when he turns round he sees that, at last, Shiherlis has caught one in the shoulder. Though he's carrying his money holdall, an automatic weapon, and a jacketload of ammo clips, McCauley goes across to Shiherlis and lifts him onto his shoulder. But after this human gesture, he becomes even more lethal. McCauley carries Shiherlis to the supermarket parking lot, while raking fire into the pedestrians, who block Hanna's way as he comes after. At one point he shoots up a barbecue display (the 'regular type life' he affected to despise). Then he hijacks an estate car and escapes spectacularly by shoving other vehicles along and reversing into unblocked roads.

Cheritto is still running alone across a concrete plaza of cafés and palm trees. Drucker and Casals are after him. He falls over in a fountain, and then sees a small girl frozen to the spot. He picks her up and uses her as a shield. But Hanna has run around the block and got ahead of him and as Cheritto turns to run ahead he is fixed in the gunsight of Hanna's powerful automatic rifle. One shot puts him dead on his back, but the child is safe. The heist music stops.

Just as we saw Eady and then Charlene, whose partners are still alive, briefly before the heist, now we see Elaine learning of Cheritto's death on the TV news at home, and Breedan's wife seeing her dead man's face on a bar's TV. Hanna's vision of death is starting to come true.

Shiherlis is hit

Cheritto goes down

Why such gun battles thrill us so must be left to the professional psychologists, but in terms of the partial mystery of this film's appeal for me, it's the battle's resemblance to one in a Western or a war film that excites me most. The Downtown gunfight plays out in a way that's exactly how small boys tend to imagine their movie-inspired made-up battles on the streets – the taking cover, the seeming invulnerability, the rescue of the pal, and the astonishing number of bullet-holes. It also echoes the tommy-gun excess of classic gangster movies. For someone who grew up in the 1960s, as I did, such made-up battles were an axiomatic part of growing up and it astounds me now to consider that I must have played war games with small gangs of kids nearly every single day for at least four years. The estate of 1930s flats I grew up in provided its own echoing canyons, but nothing quite so spectacular as this.

The remaining plot of *Heat* now plays out in a sequence of quick, doom-laden actions stretched out over a long time. McCauley is out to tidy up the mess. Having had Shiherlis's fractured clavicle seen to by a doctor, and packed him safely off to Nate, he breaks into Trejo's home, suspecting him of having ratted them out. His face registers shock as he

Trejo dies

Van Zant dies

enters the bedroom and sees what we don't see – what Waingro has done to Anna. Finding Trejo smashed up and dying on his back in a pool of blood, he learns that Waingro tortured Trejo for Van Zant. Trejo pleads with McCauley to execute him, because he's crippled and doesn't want to live on without his Anna. We see Trejo's home on stilts, overlooking those L.A. lights, and then a gunflash. Trejo, then, whose relationship was never dwelt upon, had the talent for sharing that his cohorts lacked.

McCauley is soon climbing up the poolside slope of Van Zant's Encino home. Van Zant is watching television, oblivious as a chair comes hurtling through the window. McCauley asks him where Waingro is. Van Zant says he doesn't know and gets shot several times in the chest for his trouble. That this killing is done as much to get McCauley clear of the criminal life (tidying up) as it is out of revenge laces the situation with irony.

In this supremely symmetrical film, we are here given another tour of domiciles. The cops' bank-raid tipoff has been traced to Hugh Benny, Van Zant's heavy. Hanna and Casals break into his apartment, subdue him and force him to reveal Waingro's whereabouts. Meanwhile Marciano has led Charlene and baby Dominick into a police ambush set-up in a Venice apartment. Drucker explains to her that unless Charlene agrees to sell Chris out, she will go to jail and Dominick will be taken into foster care. Charlene agrees to call him.

When McCauley comes into her apartment, Eady is disgusted with him. She tries to run away but he chases and catches her in the long grass of the hilltop as the dawn is coming up. By daybreak he is saying she can walk out if she wants to, but they are each other's only hope of romance. McCauley now is agonised. Eady looks scared and drained as if the one good thing in her life has turned poisonous. At a moment when most films would be racing for the end, Mann homes in on the personal agony of his key characters. No one seems more convinced of his irrelevance to the workings of normal society now than Vincent Hanna. When he claims back his portable TV from Justine because he finds her cooking dinner for a wimpy-looking guy named Ralph (Xander Berkeley), and then kicks the TV out of the car at a bus stop, we know his attachments are all faulty. He's become Hanna the L.A. revenant again, haunting the city at night, avoiding those moments when the life seems to drain out of him – when he's at the kitchen table.

Now comes the film's most out-and-out romantic moment. The Charlene trap is Hanna's last shot at getting McCauley before he leaves. We have seen just how dysfunctional Charlene and Shiherlis are together, but he comes when she calls. When a likely vehicle approaches, Drucker

Charlene's gesture

is warned and so he urges Charlene to show herself at the window. The camera holds on her face for a long time before she makes up her mind to move. From the balcony she sees Chris Shiherlis, with a stiff neck and his ponytail shorn off, get out of a sports car and smile up at her. She looks back at him and makes a small sideways cut with her flattened hand. He understands and departs, but not before Mann's camera has meditated in turn on their faces.

Shiherlis's no-show convinces Hanna that McCauley has gone. He decides to head back to the hotel where he's now living. He finds the bathroom flooded: Lauren is unconscious in the bath with her arms and legs slashed. He drags her out, makes tourniquets out of towels and rushes her to hospital, where Justine is waiting. The doctors save her. The subplot of Lauren's increasing misery is stretched so thinly through *Heat*, that this extensive denouement seems an elaborate way to get Hanna to face up to his own permanent deficiency as a carer.

Now heading for the escape route with Eady beside him, McCauley calls Nate for the last time. Nate tells him where Waingro is but he says he'll let it pass. Moments later, he goes through a tunnel and changes his mind.

8 Los Angeles

Below is an excerpt from an *L.A. Times* news report of a real bank raid
that happened in North Hollywood on Friday 30 April 1997, two years
after *Heat* was made. I cite it here because, first, and obviously, it
resembles *Heat*'s climactic bank job – a resemblance that so shocked TV
newscasters they constantly used it in their coverage of the event.
Second, it's a way of reintroducing the dynamic between realism and
New Hollywood opulence, and to suggest that, however implausible *Heat*
may seem, our reference points for such a judgment can shift. In Los
Angeles a term like 'realistic' can be a two-way street.

The North Hollywood Shootout
Gunfire, Hostages and Terror
By Beth Shuster and Doug Smith, L.A. Times staff writers

In warlike pursuit captured on live TV, dozens of police officers tracked down
and killed two heavily armed bank robbers in North Hollywood on Friday in
the face of blistering automatic weapons fire. Ten officers were wounded,
including six in a spectacular eruption of firepower that draped a shroud of
fear over a vast residential area ...

At least two heavily armed gunmen – suspects in an earlier San
Fernando Valley spate of bank robberies – stormed the bank about 9.15
a.m., brandishing fully automatic weapons with 100 round clips.

Barking commands, the masked gunmen herded dozens of terrified
customers into the vault.

Police said the robbers turned and fired their weapons back into the
bank, wounding one person, as they were leaving with a cart loaded with
bags of money ...

A call from a witness who saw the armored men walk into the bank
brought the first police units armed only with handguns. They were engulfed
in a gunfight, with combatants and bystanders virtually rubbing shoulders.

Crystal Ransome was leaving the bank as the gunmen entered,
pulling masks over their faces. She sought cover in her car when she heard
gun reports. 'I was laying down in my car, and the next thing I know, a cop is

telling me to "get out, get out," she said. "A cop ran me across the street. He was holding his gun drawn the whole time."

Retreating from the surrounded bank, one robber took cover behind the getaway car – a white sedan – as it crept across the parking lot, blasting away in several directions and reaching inside for ammunition to reload. At one point, he apparently fired round after round through the car window, either hitting or just missing his cohort at the wheel. Then he walked to a residential street, firing bullets along the way.[30]

According to cultural theorist Norman M. Klein,

In the United States certainly, television news increasingly is broadcast as noir cinema. News of violence is shot like hand-held incursions into neo-noir … I had students compare the television coverage [of the North Hollywood

The city at night

robbery] to scenes from *Heat*. They agreed that the movie looked more 'realistic' but, most stridently, that the film grammar was essentially identical.[31]

The robbers wore masks and body armour and seemed to think themselves as invulnerable as movie stars. The firepower they used suggests a reactive normalisation of *Heat*'s exaggeration. In L.A., it's perhaps not so surprising when life imitates art, because the city is so intertwined with its movie image.

Heat to me presents a cinematic Los Angeles whose relation to the real city is as one phantasm to another. In that sense I treat the film as an example of virtual tourism, because actual tourism – revisiting the locations of *Heat* – would make it too vulnerable to changing circumstance and mood. This approach fits with my perception of *Heat* as a meeting place for a complex set of ideas and responses that grew out of the late 1970s and the early 80s to dominate the imagery of the 1990s. In *Heat* you can find the following: an index of television cop-show lore and of neo-noir cinematography, a résumé of the careers of De Niro and Pacino, an iconography of 1980s power symbols of yuppie status and success, a tour of developments in industrial sound electronic music (another 1980s phenomenon), a political analysis of the culture of work, a summary of the career concerns of Michael Mann and, as we shall see, a very particular tour of Los Angeles. My analysis means I am falling into line with the post-modern trend among urban theorists who argue that L.A. can be used as a screen for projecting any vision you want onto it – which is exactly what Mann himself does with *Heat*.

Typical of these theorists is post-modern geographer Edward W. Soja. He argues that –

The visible aggregate of the whole of Los Angeles churns so confusingly that it induces little more than illusionary stereotypes or self-serving caricatures – if in reality it is ever seen at all. What is this place? Even knowing where to focus, to find a starting point, is not easy, for, perhaps more than any other place, Los Angeles is everywhere. It is global in the fullest sense of the world. Nowhere is this more evident than in its cultural projection and ideological reach, its almost ubiquitous screening of itself as a rectangular dream machine for the world. Los Angeles broadcasts its self-imagery so widely that probably more people have seen this place than any other on the planet.[32]

Mann's use of L.A. in *Heat* is exhaustive but cannot be definitive. He is said to have used 85 locations in and around L.A., and many of them provide the sweep of landscape, often from a high vantage point, that every Michael Mann film requires – the multi-storey car lot where McCauley meets Nate, Eady's apartment, which overlooks the 'City of Lights', Kelso's house on a hill bristling with satellite dishes, McCauley's apartment overlooking the sea, the empty drive-in movie lot where the gunfight with Van Zant's pick-up guys happens (overlooked by Shiherlis's telescopic gunsight), the dockyard where McCauley flushes out Hanna's team and photographs them from the top of a storage tank, and, inevitably, the helicopter views of Downtown at night. For Klein the film is –

clearly a homage to the denser Los Angeles ... Mann has decided to use the 'techno-industrial feel' in a more operatic way, more like his home in Chicago, the modernist encryption of skyscrapers at night ... The sprawl and deadly haze of the L.A. cloverleaf was ignored. Mann was particularly struck instead by the look of L.A. from the top of a tall building, near midnight during the smog-free season in January or February.[33]

These spacious cityscape scenes are not much in keeping with the traditional claustrophobic crime movie view of L.A. – film noir's night-town of fevered, highly sexed money-grubbers in dingy rooms. *Heat*'s sense of confinement is different. The more light-friendly neo-noir feel is down to cinematographer Dante Spinotti's ability to bring deep-etched shadows to the most sun-drenched of daytime scenes, and to his careful muting of colour constantly towards shades of grey – so that during the heist the combatants seem leeched of blood. But there are also seemingly lawless areas of L.A. that the film visits which go against Mann's upmarket villainy and are more reminiscent of Chandler and Cain's mean streets: the dog-pound and chop-shop ratrun where Torena resides, or the truck stop where the crew try to kill Waingro.

Still, it's the neo-noir world of glass cages explored in *Manhunter* that dominates: a world where you look out from a glass cell onto an immensity that you can't touch. Though I've said that the film's aesthetic follows McCauley's tastes in décor and clothes, Hanna, in the scene where he takes his TV away, refers to Justine's home as 'your ex-husband's dead-tech post-modernist bullshit house'. So the film enjoys the clean lines and daytime brilliance of such buildings but still gets in its critique – a typical Mann ambivalence. At night these are homes where the dark leaks in. Throughout *Heat* outdoor and indoor scenes have alternated as extremities. McCauley's crew and especially Hanna somehow function and think less well in interiors, and breathe more easily on the streets. It's a prison kind of claustrophobia in which everything in the cell has to be essential for survival – which is one reason why minimalism predominates.

Klein has said of *Heat*'s thieves, 'they behave like moody tourists on a tight schedule.'[34] And thinking about the constant transformations L.A. undergoes from the Soja viewpoint, the sense of the city not belonging to the thieves is even sharper if one realises how much time they will have spent away from it, in Folsom. They might have felt like Troy Cameron, the thief protagonist of Edward Bunker's 1997 novel *Dog Eat Dog*, who is released from San Quentin after more than a decade inside:

When he had gone to prison, L.A.'s vast sprawl ended at the north end of the San Fernando Valley. A few outposts of civilisation, Magic Mountain among them, were in the desert beyond the rim around the valley. Now that was the Santa Clarita Valley, and it covered the desert with tract homes, Arco gas stations, and Denny's coffee shops. The sight astounded him … Interstate 5 angled left, cutting through East L.A. Troy held to the right, up a

slope onto the inbound Pasadena Freeway. It sliced through the fields of
Elysian Park, home of the Police Academy, and when it came out of the hills
it looked at the Downtown L.A. skyline two miles away. What Troy saw was
totally different from his memory. All his life the 25 storey City Hall had risen
high above the low L.A. skyline. Now it was nearly hidden among a forest of
tall skyscrapers, nearly all built while he was gone.[35]

This vision of Downtown L.A. as a new vista and a lodestone of greed is
shared by *Heat*. 'In one scene after another,' says Klein, 'the Downtown
skyline is glowing in the background, like a pole star directing the action.
Never has the Industri-opolis looked this majestic.'[36] Just as L.A. is the
most filmed city in the world, so Downtown is its most oft-used location.
Here amid the skyscrapers is perhaps where Mann feels most at home.
But now we leave the city for the last time.

McCauley and Eady almost 'home free' (above); Waingro meets the grim reaper (below)

McCauley is still on his way out, 'home free' as Nate puts it. In the moments before he changes his mind about stopping to kill Waingro, we watch him pondering the risk to his future. 'What is it?' asks a traumatised Eady. 'Nothing,' he says, but moments later he exits the freeway, saying 'I gotta take care of something'. The conflict is visible on De Niro's face. You can see his need for vengeance outstripping his newfound belief in a 'regular type life'. At the Marquee hotel, he parks the car at a side entrance and asks Eady to wait with the engine running. He goes to the basement and apes that regular life by changing into a staff uniform. Spotting the detectives posing as lobby staff he takes the elevator to Waingro's floor, and hits a fire alarm.

He cons Waingro into opening the door and batters him backwards until he's sat on his sofa, wearing nothing but a dressing gown. 'Look at me. Look at me,' says McCauley. Waingro looks up and stares exactly like the guard stared at him before he shot him. McCauley executes him and in so doing, he releases the Waingro part of himself, returning McCauley to his original ethos. The cops have seen McCauley on a monitor and paged Hanna. One of them is waiting outside the door, but he's soon disabled and knocked unconscious. Eady, scared by the fire alarm, rubs her hands, either trying to stop them shaking or perhaps wiping away imaginary blood.

Romance in *Heat* now reaches its tragic poignancy. We've seen the agony of parting between Shiherlis and Charlene, and we've spent so much time pondering the dilemmas of McCauley and Hanna that we're perhaps wide open for pity for them and terror at their actions to coexist. Hanna has been paged but this time he's manfully ignoring the call. He and Justine are waiting in the hospital for further news of Lauren when she asks him, 'Is there any way that it could work out between us?' He says, 'I wish I could say there was but in the end … You know, it's like you said, all I have is what I'm goin' after. I'm not what you want Justine.' After a few seconds of saying she's OK, she says, 'Well go on if you want to.'

Much as one might view Hanna as a tragic figure, Justine's blessing does take the edge off it. There is, as you would expect, a fantastic tenderness to this scene. They part with fond looks and with a promise from Hanna that he will be careful and call her to say he's OK. This conversation comes close to rehabilitating Hanna. Mann's desire to have it both ways has its own double effect: the ambivalence undermines Hanna's tragic qualities, and yet it makes for a beguiling complexity.

One last chopper ride over those pinpoint lights brings Hanna to the hotel before McCauley gets out. He sees the car at a distance and seems to know that it's McCauley's. The thief is just emerging, tearing off the hotel tie (the badge of normality), when he sees Hanna. He looks at Eady and begins to back away from her, very slowly. Mann here cuts from his face to hers, from one dawning realisation to the other. McCauley is going to live out his dictum after all. He runs, Hanna follows, into pure crime genre. Only an addicted romantic would see this as anything but a kindness to Eady.

Heat's wish to contain everything that could conceivably be wrung from the coffee-shop meeting is now realised. Hanna and McCauley have become as much like our image of Pacino and De Niro as possible. The film's narrative may have condemned the foolishness of their mores, yet we share the mutual admiration of these men. Despite its integration of some sexual politics into crime genre, *Heat* never really refutes McCauley's attitude to life. Instead, it makes it an effective parody of 'me' generation attitudes: the fantasy that you can change your life at 'the drop of a hat', and walk away from difficulty. It's an appealing masculine fantasy to do with surrendering to dark impulses, of giving up the social compulsion to behave well. That's what's tragic here.

Mann's ability to balance grandeur (of scale) and austerity (of actions) makes one aware of the pleasures of coexisting opposites, of the riches that a clash between ambition and genre can lend to the crime drama. When De Niro says he's 'a needle going back to zero', or Justine says that Hanna 'searches for signs of passing', the word 'pretentious' may be on the tip of the tongue, but I won't use it. *Heat* is as realistic as it needs to be and as hyperbolic as suits a director of such aesthetic ambition.

This film is an achievement as much for its near miss at profundity as for its high score as a crime thriller. The vast resources of Hollywood

The final gunfight

have found few who can marshal them so well as Mann does here, especially in the astonishing bank-raid shoot-out. Mann works layer after layer of theme into *Heat* but it is never indigestible. The social politics are relatively discreet (though the sexual politics are anything but). The characters are vivid. The unfolding of the narrative may not always achieve the lightest of touches but ponderousness is infrequent. Mann is rare in attempting to transfer some of the principles of method acting into film direction. He says, 'I immerse myself in a film the way an actor immerses himself in a character and manipulates his immersion and accesses different parts of himself at different times.'[37] This process may sacrifice the insights of a distanced view but it produces a great deal of stunning cinema in *Heat* – a cinema of terrific texture and no small compassion that rewards several viewings.

That the final gunfight between these two dysfunctional men should take place at an airport not only reminds us of Klein's description of the crew as tourists, but it offers the contrasts of scale that are at the heart of Mann's film-making. The running figures are dwarfed by huge taxiing jets, full of regular-type people getting on with their lives, while these men seek some wide open ground in which to play out their dinosaur destiny. We still never see the two faces in the same frame. But in the sudden occasional glare of the landing lights they become giants. It is the passing of a long shadow that finally gives McCauley away to Hanna. He shoots him down. This death is mythic because the film overstates it as such, with Hanna standing rigid, holding McCauley's hand as he dies but looking away from him. It is a tribute to the dramatic force of *Heat* that we do not find the image ridiculous.

Appendix – *L.A. Takedown*

Nothing throws *Heat*'s claims to be a modern classic into more imposing relief than to watch *L.A. Takedown*, the television movie version of the same basic story made in 1989, when Mann was nearing the end of his long stint working in television. Like many another critic, I knew nothing of *L.A. Takedown* until the week of *Heat*'s release, when its existence ran as a sideline story in the British press, but the *Heat* script, in one version or another, had apparently been around since 1980. 'The earlier version [*L.A. Takedown*] was a fraction of the original screenplay,' said Mann at the time. 'It's a very superficial dress rehearsal. It was shot in 19 days – on *Heat* we had 12 days just shooting the bank robbery.'[38]

Watching *L.A. Takedown* for the first time for this book, I was expecting something light, slick and fast-moving in the *Miami Vice* vein. Instead it's a blowsy affair that takes its evocation of a flashy cop's life very seriously indeed. Here the Neil McCauley expert thief figure is called Patrick Salinko and, intriguingly, he is more sidelined as a shadow form of Hanna than equal and opposite. The friendship is less plausible: Salinko is too much of a ghost figure, a *doppelgänger* used as criminal contrast to brighten the halo around the cop's tough but heroic life.

L.A. Takedown lacks any overt sense of visual style beyond the cop-show grab-bag of fast cars and nightclubs. It is sometimes quite shockingly shambolic for a Michael Mann-branded work (he is credited as executive producer). Not only is it weakened – at least for those who see *Heat* first – by its no-budget lack of resources, but also its lead cast is made up of California mannequins rather than strong actors. This puts Mann's subsequent switch to the high-power middle-aged duo of Pacino and De Niro in an interesting light. It makes one wonder about expediency. It may have been just as essential for the television network to have bland youthful actors for *L.A. Takedown* as it was a coup that the ultimate A-list heavyweight Pacino–De Niro pairing lent their weight to the making of *Heat*. Whatever the case, for me *L.A. Takedown* has *Heat*'s hectoring tone but set to maximum power and few of its redeeming qualities. What makes it interesting for Mann-watchers is what survives of it in *Heat*, what was added and subtracted. The most intriguing element of this is just how much of the portentous dialogue is already present, and how awkward much of it sounds coming out of the mouths of pretty boys in this less prestigious context. No wonder Mann wanted a remake.

Many writers have complained that *Heat* is too slow moving. Richard Combs described it as 'an 80-minute cops and robbers drama whose parts are subjected to such minute inspection that it lasts nearly three hours'.[39] *L.A. Takedown* gives us an opportunity to see if the *Heat* script works without the minute inspection. It certainly moves at a much faster clip and leaves out nearly all of the domestic melodrama but somehow it seems more lethargic. The main differences are as follows:

- *L.A. Takedown* starts with Hanna and his wife – here named Lilian – having sex in the shower. She is childless and runs a nightclub. This relationship starts out in a healthier vein than Hanna and Justine's. It suffers only from one outburst of unnecessary violence from Hanna when he beats up a club hireling who's hitting on Lilian. This is the one scene that matches the conflict between Pacino's Hanna and Venora's Justine, including some of the dialogue used in the *Heat* scene where Hanna comes back to the empty restaurant to pick up Justine. Here Lilian echoes Justine's lines about 'what we have here is leftovers', but has different lines about their sex life being like 'a lube job, a tune-up, a pit stop'. The way the scene ends is also different: Hanna's says, 'Let's go.' She replies, 'Let's Go? There's nowhere to go.' But unlike Justine she does not end her relationship with Hanna. *L.A. Takedown* finishes with Lilian waiting outside the hotel where the bloody denouement has taken place as her victorious man emerges into her welcoming arms. This is a clear prefiguring of Brenneman waiting for McCauley at the end of *Heat*. The major change is that since Pacino's Hanna can't have the TV Hanna's domestic happiness, the waiting woman in *Heat* belongs now to the villain.

- There is no preamble setting up the armoured car job, which happens immediately pre-credits here. The third guard is executed not simply because he is witness to murder, but because he has seen Cheritto without his mask, which had fallen off. The giveaway word overheard from Cheritto is 'sport' rather than 'slick'.
- While most of the other key characters have the same names (Hanna, Cheritto, Shiherlis, Waingro), the crew leader is called Patrick Salinko rather than Neil McCauley.
- The snitch is intimidated into spilling information by Hanna alone, right at the start of the film.
- There is no Van Zant subplot – Waingro (played here with sleazy derangement by Xander Berkeley, who, in a nice irony, also plays Justine's new wimp boyfriend Ralph in *Heat*) simply turns up near the end to avenge himself by torturing the crew's driver and then ratting out the bank job to Hanna and his men.
- There is no Shiherlis and Charlene subplot. Shiherlis barely features as more than a nodding Elvis-lookalike accomplice.
- Eady is a brasher professional designer here; less of a doormouse than Brenneman plays her.
- Breedan is just there at the bank job with no back-story explanation. The scene in *Heat* where he is drinking to help him deal with the crap he has to put up with from his boss, and his wife tells him she is proud of him, is here a scene between Hanna and Lilian, where Hanna talks about 'making a difference' and Lilian says she's proud of him.
- There is no abandoned precious metals robbery, Cheritto finds the bugs in his car and warns the crew that the LAPD is on to them.
- The coffee-shop meeting between Hanna and Salinko is not set up; it happens by chance, they bump into one another in the parking lot.
- Salinko does not kill Waingro. Hanna and his men hold Salinko up just as he is about to storm Waingro's door. Waingro sends a shotgun blast through the door fatally wounding Salinko. So *L.A.*

Takedown's denouement is not the tragic *pietà*-like one of McCauley dying while holding Hanna's hand but rather Hanna kicking Waingro out through his apartment window to his death on the concrete below, followed by Hanna's reconciliation with Lilian.

If we look at what's missing from *L.A. Takedown*, we find that some substantial parts have had their own dress rehearsal. The Van Zant subplot is very similar to the double-crossing of Frank in *Thief*, even down to some of the detail of the money exchange overlooked by the crewman with a telescopic rifle. This tends to back up Mann's claim that *L.A. Takedown* is a deliberate dry run. Throughout Mann's career there has been evidence of the trying out and recycling of ideas. There's an episode of *Miami Vice*, for instance, in which star cop Sonny Crockett takes on the role of the 'empath' psychological profiler sensing what happened in a brutal 'home invasion' case in exactly the same way that Will Graham does in *Manhunter*.

L.A. Takedown reveals how important resources of such a huge scale are to *Heat*. We miss the thrill of authentic automatic gunfire, of swooping helicopters, of expensive speeding roadsters and inexorable trucks; in considering these elements we again come back to how much of a procedural thriller *Heat* is, how much the suspenseful exposition of incident has to punch its weight with the stuff of high drama crammed in between.

More intriguingly *L.A. Takedown* also gives us clues as to the transition that took Mann from *Miami Vice*, with its over-determined *mise en scène* of high-flash fashion, of pretty boys in pastel satins, to the sombre seriousness of *Heat*. *Takedown* is more like *Vice* in its reliance on the plastic virtues of model looks and disco beats. In that sense it may just be reflecting the requirements of the TV networks and of the dynamics of building up to ad breaks and keeping viewer's fingers from straying to the zapper. On the other hand we can also see how overbearing *L.A. Takedown*'s themes seem in a TV context. The benefit of hindsight makes us crave the larger canvas of *Heat*.

Notes

1 See J. A. Lindstrom, 'Heat: Work and Genre', *Jump Cut* no. 43, 2000, p. 21.
2 See Richard Combs, 'Michael Mann: Becoming', *Film Comment*, vol. 32 no. 2, March/April 1996, p. 10.
3 Lindstrom, 'Heat: Work and Genre', p. 24.
4 See *Melville on Melville*, ed. by Rui Nogueira (London: Secker and Warburg, 1971), p. 155.
5 See Graham Fuller, 'Michael Mann', *Interview*, December 1995, p. 36.
6 See Tom Shone, 'The Man Who Shot Al and Bob', *Sunday Times*, 21 January 1996, *The Culture* supplement, pp. 6–7.
7 See Fred Schruers, 'Mann Overboard', *Premiere*, October 1992, p. 60.
8 See Gavin Smith, 'Wars and Peace', *Sight and Sound* vol. 7 no. 2, November 1992, p. 10.
9 See Lynn Hirschberg, 'Michael Mann', *Rolling Stone,* 17 December 1987, p. 163.
10 See United Artists press notes for *Thief*, undated.
11 See John Patterson, 'Crime and Punishment', *Guardian*, 26 April 2002, *Friday Review* section, p. 5.
12 See Michael Sragow, 'Michael Mann', *Rolling Stone*, 14 May 1981, p. 35.
13 See Geoff Andrew,'Esprit de Corpse', *Time Out*, 15 February 1989, p. 20.
14 See Pauline Kael, *Movie Love* (London: Marion Boyars, 1992), p. 262.
15 See Walter Goodman, 'Manhunter', *New York Times*, 15 August 1986, p. 32.
16 See Combs, *Monthly Film Bulletin*, vol. 66 no. 661, February 1989, pp. 52–3.
17 Andrew, 'Esprit de Corpse', p. 21.
18 Schruers, 'Mann Overboard', p. 70.
19 See Richard T. Jameson, 'Men over Miami', *Film Comment* vol. 21 no. 2, March/April 1985, p. 66.

20 See Geoff Andrew, 'Mann to Man', *Time Out*, 17 January 1996, pp. 16–17.
21 See Smith, 'Wars and Peace', p. 12.
22 See David Hare, 'Why Fabulate?', *Guardian*, *Saturday Review* section 2 February 2002, p. 3.
23 Andrew, 'Mann to Man', pp. 16–17.
24 Ibid.
25 See Robert Warshow, 'The Gangster as Tragic Hero', in *The Immediate Experience* (New York: Doubleday, 1962), pp. 127–33.
26 Website interview, now deleted.
27 Between 1979 and 1981 six issues of a London art/fashion/style magazine called *ZG* (standing, of course, for zeitgeist) were published, straddling the creative aftermath of punk. Though it was produced in London, its spiritual home was New York. As might be expected, it is postmodern in its outlook. Knowing that Michael Mann first conceived of *Heat* in that period it is curious to discover how much of the eventual aesthetic of the film can be traced back to the cultural concerns of that time. *ZG*'s articles are not very impressive in retrospect but their range of reference is an exciting reminder of a time of creative ferment. In particular, the post-punk era is the moment when the influence of French theorists really came through in the Anglo-Saxon countries. The articles of *ZG* are full of half-digested Baudrillardian and Barthesian angles on art, architecture and street culture. The big excitement was the symbiotic feeding frenzy going on between street and gallery art (graffiti), between disco and avant-garde musics (Ze records); punk and avant-garde musics (N. Y. Noise music); and between street and formal fashion. It is this street aspiration for high art glamour (New Romantics) and its inverse, the uptown

need for downtown grit (for instance, the financial centres' need for quick-witted, aggressive 'street smart' types as traders), that mark the 1980s out from the 70s. A similar tension also informs the aesthetic of *Heat*. In this super-production, every character, whether cop or criminal, seems to aspire to an 80s idea of the good life. The New York special issue of *ZG* was the third published in 1981 (*ZG* was an irregular publication, more easily found in clothes shops than in newsagents), and, looking back, it seems particularly predictive of how *Heat* would look and sound with articles on the aestheticisation of consumption, Robert Longo's artworks, Glenn Branca's guitar orchestra and Bloomingdale's catalogue.

28 See Ian Nathan, 'Hey Let's Be Careful Out There …', *Empire*, March 1996, p. 86.
29 See Peter Guttridge, 'The Controller General', *Independent*, 18 April 1996, section 2, pp. 10–11.
30 See Beth Shuster and Doug Smith, 'The North Hollywood Shootout', *L.A. Times Home Edition*, 1 March 1997, p. A1.
31 See Norman M. Klein, 'Gold Fevers: Global L.A. and the Noir Imaginary', in *Reading California: Art, Image and Identity, 1900–2000* (Los Angeles: Los Angeles County Museum of Art/University of California Press, 2000), p. 397.
32 See Edward W. Soja, *Postmodern Geographies: The Reassertion of Space in Critical Social Theory* (London: Verso, 1989), pp. 222–3.
33 See Norman M. Klein, *The History of Forgetting: Los Angeles and the Erasure of Memory* (London: Verso, 1997) p. 110.
34 Ibid. p. 111.
35 See Edward Bunker, *Dog Eat Dog* (London: No Exit Press, 2000), p. 83.
36 Klein, *The History of Forgetting*, p. 110.
37 Smith, 'Wars and Peace', p. 14.
38 See Geoffrey Macnab, 'Heist Almighty!', *Time Out*, 22 December 1999, p. 183.
39 Combs, 'Michael Mann: Becoming', p. 10.

Credits

HEAT

USA
1995

Directed by
Michael Mann
Produced by
Michael Mann, Art Linson
Written by
Michael Mann
Director of Photography
Dante Spinotti
Edited by
Dov Hoenig, Pasquale
Buba, William Goldenberg,
Tom Rolf
Production Designer
Neil Spisak
Music Composed by
Elliot Goldenthal

©Monarchy Enterprises B.V.
and Regency Entertainment
(USA) Inc

Production Companies
Warner Bros. presents in
association with Regency
Enterprises
a Forward Pass production
a Michael Mann film
Executive Producers
Arnon Milchan,
Pieter Jan Brugge
Associate Producers
Kathleen M. Shea,
Gusmano Cesaretti
Production Accountant
Cheryl A. Stone
**Assistant Production
Accountants**
Michael R. Kern,
Edward Allen
**Production Office
Co-ordinator**
Sharyn Shimada-Huggins
**Assistant Production
Co-ordinators**
Michael Dean Valeo,
Marc A. Hammer
Unit Production Manager
Christopher Cronyn
Location Managers
Janice Polley, Lori A. Balton
**Assistant Location
Managers**
Andrew L. Ullman, Ralph
Coleman, Peter Martorano,
Mike Fantasia
**Post-production
Supervisors**
Kathy Virkler, Mark Stevens

**Office Production
Assistants**
Al Lewis, Samantha Roth,
Brian Spain, Venessa
Verdugo
Set Production Aides
Jonathan McGarry, Jody
Spilkoman, Tendaji Lathan,
David Hyman, Josiah W.
Hooper, Casey B. Collins,
Selma Kora
**Production Office
Secretary**
Shannon Hamed
**Assistant to Michael
Mann**
Carlo Bernard
**Executive Assistant to
Michael Mann**
Michelle Fielding
**Assistants to Pieter Jan
Brugge**
Jamie D. Boscardin,
Ami Canaan Mann
Assistant to Art Linson
Patty Roberts Nelson
Staff Assistants
Debra Puopolo,
Andy Walraven, Jeff Berger,
Ron Senkowski
Assistants to Mr Pacino
Lou Crisa, Tim Judge
Assistant to Mr De Niro
Robin Chambers
Assistant to Mr Kilmer
Jane Payne
Second Unit Director
Ami Canaan Mann
First Assistant Director
Michael Waxman

Second Assistant Director
Douglas S. Ornstein

2nd Second Assistant Director
Julie Herrin

DGA Trainee
Rich Sickler

Script Supervisor
Cate Hardman

Casting by
Bonnie Timmermann

Casting Associate
Alison E. McBryde

Extras Casting
Tammy L. Smith

Casting Assistant
Cynthia Ellis

Camera Operator
Gary Jay

Steadicam Operator/ 'B' Camera
James Muro

First Assistant Camera
Duane 'DC' Manwiller,
Chris Moseley

Second Assistant Camera
David Galbraith, Kelsey
'Kshaw' McNeal

Loader
James Apted

Key Grip
W. C. 'Chunky' Huse

Best Boy Grip
Daniel Haizlip

Dolly Grip
Gerrit Garretsen

Rigging Grip
Andrew Taylor

Chief Lighting Technician
Jim Grce

Assistant Chief Lighting Technician
David R. Christensen

Rigging Gaffer
Frank Dorowsky

Still Photography
Frank Connor

Visual Effects Supervisor
Neil Krepela

Digital Compositing by
Pacific Title Digital

Digital Effects Producer
Joe Gareri

Digital Effects Supervisor
David Sosalla

Digital Effects Artists
Patrick Phillips, Mimi Abers,
John La Fauce

Special Effects Co-ordinator
Terry D. Frazee

Special Effects Foreman
Donald Frazee

Special Effects
Geno Crum, Logan Frazee,
Donald Myers, Ralph
Winiger, Bruce Y. Kuroyama,
Paul H. Haines Jr,
Rick Monak

24 Frame Video Operator
Larry Markart

Video Assist
Steven Mikolas

First Assistant Film Editors
Vicki Hiatt, Matthew Booth,
Ray Boniker, Tom Bryant

Assistant Film Editors
Andrea Bottigliero, John
Morrisey, Kristina Trirogoff,
Mark Westmore, David
Dresher

Electronic Assistant Film Editors
Nina Lucia, Lynn Leonhard,
Julie Janata, Sondra
Watanabe, Andi Kasen
Van Kirk

Negative Cutter
Mo Henry

Art Director
Marjorie Stone McShirley

Art Department Co-ordinator
L. Oscar A. Mazzola

Assistant Art Department Co-ordinator
Alexandra Milchan

Assistant Art Director
Dianne Wager

Set Designers
Robert Fectman,
Steven Schwartz,
Paul Sonski

Lead
Douglas E. Maxwell,
Charles R. Lipscomb,
Nigel A. Boucher

Set Decorator
Anne H. Ahrens

Illustrator
Sean Hargreaves

Storyboard Artist
Jeff Balsmeyer

Set Dressers
Amy Beth Feldman, Ross Harpold, David Hopkins, James T. Randol, Brad Curry, Robyn B. Holmes
Construction Co-ordinator
Anthony Lattanzio
Construction Foremen
Mike Sforza, Scott Hanson
Paint Foreman
Larry Clark
Sign Painter
Joe A. Hawthorne
Stand-by Painter
John Hinkle
Labour Foreman
Rick Hausfeld
Greens Foreman
Philip C. Hurst
Property Master
Charles Stewart
Assistant Property Masters
Amie Frances McCarthy, Teri Anne Kopp
Costume Designer
Deborah L. Scott
Assistant Costume Designer
David Le Vey
Costume Supervisor
Darryl M. Athons
Costumers
Priscilla B. Poore, Tom Numbers, Beth Koenigsberg, Lillian Lanette Little
Mr Pacino's Costumer
Joseph T. Mastrolia

Mr De Niro's Costumer
Marsha Bozeman
Mr Kilmer's Costumer
Brenda Donoho
Key Make-up Artist
John Caglione Jr
Make-up Artist & Tattoo Designer
Ken Diaz
Mr De Niro's Make-up & Hair
Ilona Herman
Mr Kilmer's Make-up & Hair
Leonard Engleman
Key Hairstylist
Vera Mitchell
Hairstylist
Timothy Jones
Design & Animation of Main Title Sequence by
Research Arts, London
Titles and Opticals by
Pacific Title
Colour Timer
David Orr
Music Score Performances by
The Kronos Quartet
Conducted by
Jonathan Sheffer, Stephen Mercurio
Orchestrated by
Robert Elhai, Elliot Goldenthal
Music Supervisor
Budd Carr
Assistant Music Supervisor
Amy Dunn

Music Consultant
Chris Douridas
Music Adviser
Curt Sobel
Music Score Produced by
Matthias Gohl
Electronic Score Produced by
Richard Martinez
Supervising Music Editors
Bill Abbott, Christopher Brooks
Music Editors
Lee Scott, Stephen Lotwis, Michael Connell, Jay Richardson, Denise Okimoto
Score Recorded and Mixed by
Stephen McLaughlin, Joel Iwataki
Soundtrack
'Always Forever Now' by/performed by Passengers (Brian Eno, U2); 'Late Evening in Jersey' by/performed by Brian Eno; 'Last Nite' by Terje Rypdal, performed by Terje Rypdal & The Chasers; 'Force Marker' by/performed by Brian Eno; 'New Dawn Fades' by Ian Curtis, Peter Hook, Bernard Sumner, Stephen Morris, performed by Moby; 'Mystery Man' by/performed by Terje Rypdal; 'God Moving over

the Face of the Waters' by Richard Hall, performed by Moby; 'The Monkey King' by/ performed by William Orbit; 'Gringatcho Demento' by William Orbit, Cleo Torez, performed by William Orbit; 'The Last Lagoon', 'The Mighty Limpopo' by/performed by William Orbit; 'Arabic Agony' by Timothy Booth, Lawrence Gott, James Glennie, Brian Eno, performed by James; 'Ultramarine' by/performed by Michael Brook; 'La bas', 'Celon', 'Gloradin' by/performed by Lisa Gerrard; 'In November' by/performed by David Darling; 'Armenia' by/performed by Einsturzende Neubauten; 'Black Cloud' by Steve Roach, Elmar Schulte, performed by Solitaire; 'Will Gaines' by/performed by Eric Clapton; 'The Thrill Is Gone' by Roy Hawkins, Rick Darnell, performed by B. B. King; 'Top o' the Morning to Ya' by Erik Schrody, Leor Dimant, Willie Dixon, performed by House of Pain; 'By the Time I Get to Phoenix' by Jimmy Webb; 'Concerto for Violoncello and Orchestra' by György Ligeti, performed by Jean-Guihen Queyras and The Ensemble InterContemporain, conducted by Pierre Boulez; 'Get Up to This' by Derrick Gumbus, Loren Chaney, performed by New World Beat

Soundtrack Album on
Warner Bros. Records CDs and Tapes

Production Sound Mixer
Lee Orloff

Sound by
SoundDeLux

Utility Sound
Thomas A. Payne

Additional Audio
Kim Waugh

Boom Operator
Nicholas R. Allen

Supervising Sound Editors
Per Hallberg, Larry Kemp

First Assistant Sound Editor
Karen M. Baker

Assistant Sound Editors
Greg Plotts, Judson Leach, Bob Bowman, Horace Manzanares, Tim Groseclose, Ann Fisher, Philip Morrill

Dialogue Editors
Dan M. Rich, Lauren Stevens, Neil Anderson, Hector Gika, Duncan Burns

Re-recording Mixers
Chris Jenkins, Andy Nelson, Ron Bartlett, Anna Behlmer, Mark Smith, John Arrias

Additional Re-recording Mixers
Gary Alexander, Dan Leahy, Ken S. Polk, Robert Thirlwell, Doug Hemphill, Chris Carpenter, Bill Benton, Bill Jackson

Re-recorded at
Todd-AO

FX Editors
Richard Dwan Jr, Christopher Assells, Peter Michael Sullivan, Mark Lapointe, Scott Gershin, Alan Rankin, Randy Kelley, Rick Bozeat, Mark Stoeckinger, Pete Lehman, Brian McPherson, Dave McMoyler, Rick Morris

ADR Supervisor
Joe Mayer

ADR Editors
Mary Ruth Smith, Lou Kleinman, Cliff Latimer, Holly Huckins, Zack Davis

Foley Artists
Ellen Heuer, Chris Moriana

Foley Mixer
David Jobe

Foley Editors
Clint Hegeman, Stuart Copely, Mark Gordon, Philip Hess

Technical Advisers
Charles Adamsom, Tom Elfmont, Gil Parra, Rey Verdugo

Technical Weapons Training
Mick Gould, Andy McNab

Technical Support
Richard Smedley,
Foxtrot Productions Ltd
Transportation
Co-ordinator
Bryce Guy Williams
Transportation Captains
Howard Bachrach,
Steve Duncan
Medics
Russ Tanaka, Tammy Kalka
Catering
Gala Catering
Craft Service
Chris Winn, Rich Cody
Stunt Co-ordinator
Joel Kramer
Stunts
Doug Coleman,
Cliff McLaughlin, Tom Elliott,
Norman Howell, Gary
McLarty, Chuck Tamburro,
Tony Brubaker,
John Tamburro
Unit Publicist
Peter Haas
Camera Dollies
Provided by
J. L. Fisher
Camera Cranes and
Dollies Provided by
Chapman
Infracam Thermal
Camera Provided by
Inframetrix
Electronic Surveillance
Equipment Provided by
Litton Electronics
F.L.I.R. Unit Provided by
F.L.I.R. Systems, Inc

CNN News Footage
Provided by
CNN ©Cable News
Network, Inc
KFWB News Courtesy of
KFWB-AM, Los Angeles,
CA, a CBS station
KNBC-TV News Footage
Courtesy of
KNBC-TV
KTTV News Footage
Courtesy of
KTTV News
The Producers Wish to
Thank the Following
City of Los Angeles,
The Entertainment Industry
Development Corporation,
Los Angeles Film Office,
State of California, California
Film Commission, Cal
Trans, California Highway
Patrol, City of Santa Monica
and Its Citizens, Los
Angeles International
Airport, Far East National
Bank, The Los Angeles
Police Department, The Los
Angeles County Sheriff's
Department, California
Department of Corrections,
Folsom State Prison,
California State Prison
Sacramento, Peter J.
Pitchess Honor Rancho,
North County Correctional
Facility, The Pelican Bay
Information Project, Legal
Services for Prisoners with
Children, AMS NEVE

Cast
Al Pacino
Vincent Hanna
Robert De Niro
Neil McCauley
Val Kilmer
Chris Shiherlis
Tom Sizemore
Michael Cheritto
Diane Venora
Justine
Amy Brenneman
Eady
Dennis Haysbert
Donald Breedan
Ashley Judd
Charlene Shiherlis
Mykelti Williamson
Sergeant Drucker
Wes Studi
Casals
Ted Levine
Danny Bosko
William Fichtner
Roger Van Zant
Natalie Portman
Lauren Gustafson,
Justine's daughter
Tom Noonan
Kelso
Kevin Gage
Waingro
Hank Azaria
Alan Marciano
Susan Traylor
Elaine Cheritto
Kim Staunton
Lillian
Jon Voight
Nate

Danny Trejo
Trejo
Henry Rollins
Hugh Benny
Jerry Trimble
Schwartz
Marty Ferrero
construction clerk
Ricky Harris
Albert Torena
Tone Lōc
Richard Torena
Begonya Plaza
Anna Trejo
Hazelle Goodman
hooker's mother
Ray Buktenica
Timmons
Jeremy Piven
Dr Bob
Xander Berkeley
Ralph
Rick Avery
armoured guard 2
Brad Baldridge
children's hospital doctor
Andrew Camuccio
Brian Camuccio
Dominick
Max Daniels
shooter at drive-in
Vince Deadrick Jr
driver at drive-in
Charles Duke
cop 5
Thomas Elfmont
desk clerk cop
Kenny Endoso
bartender
Kimberly Flynn
Casals' date

Steven Ford
Officer Bruce
Farrah Forke
Claudia
Hannes Fritsch
Miracle Mile bartender
Amanda Graves
Linda Cheritto
Emily Graves
Anita Cheritto
Niki Harris
Marcia Drucker
Ted Harvey
detective 2
Patricia Healy
Bosko's date
Paul Herman
Sergeant Heinz
Cindy Katz
Rachel
Brian Libby
Captain Jackson
Bill McIntosh
armoured guard 1
Dan Martin
Harry Dieter
Rick Marzan
basketball player
Terry Miller
children's hospital nurse
Paul Moyer
news anchorman
Daniel O'Haco
detective 1
Mario Roberts
bank guard 1
Phillip Robinson
Alphonse
Thomas Rosales Jr
armoured truck driver

Rainell Saunders
dead hooker
Kai Soremekun
prostitute
Rey Verdugo
Vegas cop
Wendy L. Walsh
news anchorwoman
Yvonne Zima
hostage girl

[uncredited]
Bud Cort
Solenko, coffee-shop
manager

Dolby Digital/SDDS
Colour/Prints by
Technicolor
2.35:1 [Panavision]

15,362 feet
171 minutes

MPAA: 34160

Credits compiled by
Markku Salmi,
BFI Filmographic Unit

Also Published

L'Argent
Kent Jones (1999)

Blade Runner
Scott Bukatman (1997)

Blue Velvet
Michael Atkinson (1997)

Caravaggio
Leo Bersani & Ulysse Dutoit
(1999)

A City of Sadness
Bérénice Reynaud (2002)

Crash
Iain Sinclair (1999)

The Crying Game
Jane Giles (1997)

Dead Man
Jonathan Rosenbaum
(2000)

Don't Look Now
Mark Sanderson (1996)

Do the Right Thing
Ed Guerrero (2001)

**Dilwale Dulhaniya Le
Jayenge**
Anupama Chopra (2002)

Easy Rider
Lee Hill (1996)

Eyes Wide Shut
Michel Chion (2002)

The Exorcist
Mark Kermode (1997,
2nd edn 1998)

Heat
Nick James (2002)

Independence Day
Michael Rogin (1998)

Jaws
Antonia Quirke (2002)

Last Tango in Paris
David Thompson (1998)

**Once Upon a Time in
America**
Adrian Martin (1998)

Pulp Fiction
Dana Polan (2000)

The Right Stuff
Tom Charity (1997)

**Saló or The 120 Days of
Sodom**
Gary Indiana (2000)

Seven
Richard Dyer (1999)

The Silence of the Lambs
Yvonne Tasker (2002)

The Terminator
Sean French (1996)

Thelma & Louise
Marita Sturken (2000)

The Thing
Anne Billson (1997)

**The 'Three Colours'
Trilogy**
Geoff Andrew (1998)

Titanic
David M. Lubin (1999)

Trainspotting
Murray Smith (2002)

The Usual Suspects
Ernest Larsen (2002)

The Wings of the Dove
Robin Wood (1999)

**Women on the Verge of a
Nervous Breakdown**
Peter William Evans (1996)

**WR – Mysteries of the
Organism**
Raymond Durgnat (1999)